H.P. LOVECRAFT

AGAINST THE WORLD,
AGAINST LIFE

by MICHEL HOUELLEBECQ

TRANSLATED FROM THE FRENCH
by DORNA KHAZENI

WITH AN INTRODUCTION
by STEPHEN KING

First published in 1991 as H. P. Lovecraft: Contre le monde,
contre le vie by Editions du Rocher. All rights reserved.

First published in Great Britain in 2006 by
Weidenfeld & Nicholson

This edition published in Great Britain
in 2008 by Gollancz
An imprint of the Orion Publishing Group
Orion House, 5 Upper St Martin's Lane, London WC2H 9EA

An Hachette Livre UK Company

11

A CIP catalogue record for this book is available
from the British Library

ISBN 978 0 575 08401 8

Printed in Great Britain by
CPI Group (UK) Ltd, Croydon, CR0 4YY

www.orionbooks.co.uk

The Orion Publishing Group's policy is to use papers that
are natural, renewable and recyclable products and made
from wood grown in sustainable forests. The logging and
manufacturing processes are expected to conform to the
environmental regulations of the country of origin.

H. P. LOVECRAFT

AGAINST THE WORLD,
AGAINST LIFE

TABLE OF CONTENTS

"LOVECRAFT'S PILLOW"

by STEPHEN KING

Michel Houellebecq's longish essay *H. P. Lovecraft: Against the World, Against Life* is a remarkable blending of critical insight, fierce partisanship, and sympathetic biography—a kind of scholarly love letter, maybe even the world's first truly cerebral mash note. The question is whether or not the subject rates such a rich and unexpected burst of creativity in what is ordinarily a dull-as-ditchwater, footnote-riddled field of work. Does this long-dead, pulp-magazine Johnson deserve such a Boswell? Houellebecq argues that H. P. Lovecraft does, that he matters a great deal even in the twenty-first century.

As it happens, I think he could not be more right.

Have you ever scared yourself?
Here's a question every writer whose work has touched upon the weird, the supernatural, or the macabre has been asked, not once but many times. I am sure that H. P. Lovecraft faced the query, and that he replied with his customary gravity and *politesse* no matter how many times he heard it. Certainly he would never have answered as did one writer at a World Horror Convention I attended some years ago, with another question: *Have I ever taken a piss?*

Vulgar, that, but otherwise not a bad response. Because *any* writer who has worked this field of literature more than occasionally has scared him or herself. Men who've spent their lives in coal mines cough. Guitarists have calluses on the tips of their fingers. Deskmen and women often walk with a pronounced stoop by the time they reach middle age. These are occupational hazards. For the horror writer, the occasional scare when the imagination performs especially well is another. It comes with the territory, and most of us who work that territory consider a passing *frisson* no more interesting than the coal miner considers his cough, or the guitarist the tough spots on the ends of her fingers.

There is, however, a related question. Ask a group of writers who have specialized in tales of horror and the supernatural if they've ever had an idea too scary even to write about, and their eyes will light up. Then you're no longer talking about occupational hazards, which is boring; then you're *talking shop*, which is never boring.

I've had at least one such idea. It came to me while I was attending my first World Fantasy Convention, in the dim and antique year of 1979. That WorldCon happened to be held in Providence, HPL's hometown. While wandering aimlessly about on Saturday afternoon (and wondering, of course, if Lovecraft had once wandered the same streets), I happened to pass a pawnshop. The window was crowded with the usual bright assortment of goods: electric guitars, clock radios, straight razors, saxophones, rings, pendants, and guns-guns-guns.

While I was looking in at all this rickrack, Mr. Idea Man spoke up from his Barcalounger at the back of my head, as he sometimes does, and for reasons no writer seems to fully understand.[1] Mr. Idea Man said, "What if there was a pillow in that window? Just

---

[1] I have said, on one occasion or another, that the "I have an idea for a story" moment comes

an ordinary old pillow in a slightly dirty cotton slip? And suppose somebody curious about why such an item would be on display—a writer like you, maybe—went in and asked about it, and the guy who ran the pawnshop said it was H. P. Lovecraft's pillow, the one he slept on every night, the one he dreamed his fantastic dreams on,[2] maybe even the one he died on."

Reader, I cannot remember—even now, a quarter-century later—ever having an idea that gave me such a chill. Lovecraft's pillow! The one that cradled his narrow head when he left consciousness behind! And "Lovecraft's Pillow" would, of course, be the title of my story. I hurried back to my hotel fully intending to skip everything else I had planned, two panel discussions and a dinner, in order to write it. By the time I arrived, a great many details about that pillow had come clear in my mind. I could see the slightly yellowish cast of the cloth; I could see a ghostly, brownish ring that might have been a tiny leakage of spittle from the corner of the thin-lipped, sleeping mouth; I could see a dot of darker brown that was surely blood which had slipped from one nostril.

And I could hear the low squeal of the dreams trapped inside. Yes indeed. The chittering of H. P. Lovecraft's nightmares.

If I had started the story right away, as I'd planned, I'm almost sure it would have been written, but as I was walking down the twelfth-floor corridor to my room, some hilarious soul popped out of another room, slapped a beer in my hand, and pulled me into a group of happy, promiscuously talking writers. Then came the panel discussions (after all), and the dinner (naturally), followed by a great deal more drinking (of course) and talking (to be sure).

---

when very common things are perceived in an entirely new way, or in some new configuration. That usually shuts people up because it sounds plausible. It *is* plausible, and it *is* part of the "I have an idea" moment, but there's more to it. I just can't explain what the more is, even after all these years. I *can* say that it sometimes feels like being shot in the brain.

[2] For more on Lovecraft's dreams, many of which became part of his stories, see Houellebecq.

Not a little of the talk was about HPL, and I participated gladly, but I never *did* write that story.

Later that night, in bed, my mind turned to it again, and what had seemed marvelous in the afternoon light became awful to think about in the dark. It was thinking of *his* stories, you see—the ones that had been in that narrow head, horrors separated from the pillow by only the thinnest shield of bone. The best of them—what Michel Houellebecq calls "the great texts"—are uniquely terrible in all of American literature, and survive with all their power intact. Lovecraft's only stylistic rival at mid-twentieth century, ironically enough, may have been the *noir* writer David Goodis, whose language was entirely different but who shared Lovecraft's inability to ever *stop,* to say enough is *enough,* but had that neurotic need to simply keep drilling away at the column of reality. Goodis, however, has fallen into obscurity. Lovecraft never did. And why not? I think because, unlike Goodis, the shrill pitch of HPL's compulsion was balanced by a kind of lumbering poetry and an unearthly range of imaginative vision. His screams of horror are *lucid.*

And was I, I wondered as I lay sleepless upon my own pillow, actually going to try and put all that into a story? The idea was ludicrous. To try and fail would be miserable. To try and succeed would require an expenditure of psychic energy—not to mention simple nerve—far beyond what any short story (save perhaps one by Gogol... or Lovecraft himself) deserved. And the idea of trying to maintain such a gruesome conceit for the duration of a novel, even a short one, was too daunting for serious consideration. I felt like a would-be diver on the cliffs at Acapulco, who probably would have been all right if he'd just gone ahead and jumped after a cursory look to make sure he was on the right side of the rocks. Instead, I paused too long to consider the drop and the possible consequences. Thus was I lost.

"Lovecraft's Pillow" wasn't written that weekend in Providence, and has never been written since. If you would like to try your hand at it, Reader, I bequeath it to you… not to mention the bad dreams that are sure to follow any serious effort to do such a thing justice. As for myself, I no longer want to go inside Lovecraft's pillow, to visit whatever dreams may remain caught there, and I have an idea that's a point of view with which Michel Houellebecq could sympathize.

In his very unacademic passion, Houellebecq makes assertions which will cause controversy and start arguments. I dispute some of them myself. *Is* life painful and disappointing? The former may be true, but only at times; the latter may be true, but only for some people. *Is* it useless to write new realistic novels? About two thousand pages of prose over the last fourteen years suggests that Tom Wolfe, at least, would beg to differ. *Does* humanity inspire only attenuated curiosity in us? Ah, my dear Houellebecq! Each day I meet at least sixty people and long to follow forty of them home in order to see what they do there.

There are other assertions, perhaps the most controversial having to do with Lovecraft's supposed disinterest in sex and dismissal of Freud,[3] but we must pass them by without extended discussion—if this introduction runs too long, it will overwhelm the book that follows! Besides, Houellebecq's argument that Lovecraft was one of the most important American writers of the twentieth century, while not beyond debate, becomes less dismissible with every passing decade that his books remain in print and his works

---

[3] It can be argued that such "great texts" as "The Dunwich Horror" and "At the Mountains of Madness" are about sex and little else, and that when Cthulhu makes one of its appearances in Lovecraft's tales, we are witnessing a gigantic, tentacle-equipped, killer vagina from beyond space and time. I'm not trying to make light of HPL, only pointing out that if the Elder Gods are seen from a psychoanalytic standpoint, especially from the standpoint of psychoanalysis as it existed in HPL's time, then we're in a Freudian three-ring circus.

become more widely taught in the literature courses of America and the world beyond. And Lovecraft's *literary* importance may be secondary to the fact—attested to by the very passion of Michel Houellebecq's essay—that HPL continues to remain not just *popular* with generation after generation of maturing readers but *viscerally important* to an imaginative core group that goes on to write that generation's fantasy and weird tales… and, by so doing, to chart that generation's deepest fears. I'm no fan of sociological analysis when it comes to literature, but I think that a generation's weird fiction, which has always been mainstream literature's first cousin (and sometimes its twin sister), gives us valuable information about the society in which it appears. If you show us what terrified a generation (the nightmares inside the national pillow, if you like), then nine times out of ten a great many other decisions that were made during the time that fiction was being published— legal, moral, economic, even military—come into perfect focus.

But put all that psychological and sociological business aside. It's mostly twaddle, make-work for spies in the house of literature, those chickenshit academics (their number grows yearly) who will grasp at any straw to keep from talking about story and language and imagination—the sweet DNA of fiction—because it makes them uncomfortable, leaves them with the all-too-real possibility of a fifty-minute class where they have almost no lecture notes and so the *real* horrors loom: dead air and staring student eyes.

Whatever bones to pick I may have with some of Michel Houellebecq's conclusions and assumptions, I never once doubted his central thesis, that Lovecraft's works stand against the world and against life. As both a reader of weird fiction and as one who has written my share, I understood at once that Houellebecq had written something I'd long felt but had never been able to express— that weird fiction, fiction of horror and the supernatural, utters a resounding *NO* to the world as it is and reality as the world insists it must be. And (Houellebecq doesn't state this in so many words, but his very admiration of Lovecraft proclaims it, shouts it from the rooftops) the *greater the imagination* and *the stronger the connection between writer and reader,* the more emphatic and persuasive that *NO* becomes. Houellebecq expresses the technique necessary to achieve such an adamant shout in piecemeal subheads, and it will perhaps not hurt his overall purpose to assemble them here:

Attack the story like a radiant suicide, utter the great NO to life without weakness; then you will see a magnificent cathedral, and your senses, vectors of unutterable derangement, will map out an integral delirium that will be lost in the unnameable architecture of time.

For the would-be writer of weird fiction, it is indispensable advice.[4] For the reader approaching Lovecraft for the first time, it—and Houellebecq's essay, in which it is embedded—is a useful touchstone, a way of understanding how Lovecraft proceeded. As to how Lovecraft *succeeded*—that is a mystery no book, essay, or university seminar will ever unravel. That is between each reader and the Lovecraft he or she discovers, the one who opens each reader's imagination with those long, drilling passages that seem to scream... and then to become a voice that whispers late at night, when sleep won't come and the moon peers coldly in the window.

The voice whispering from inside the pillow.

A portion of young readers in each generation comes to Lovecraft without prompting or guidance, just as a portion of each generation comes to Agatha Christie... and Stoker's *Dracula*... and will, I suspect, come to the *Harry Potter* books for years or even centuries to come. What sets Lovecraft apart and makes him worthy of this fiery, fiercely partisan essay isn't so much literary merit—oh, such a slippery term—as his brute staying power. Unlike

---

[4] Although easier said than done. Take it from one who knows.

Christie or Stoker or Rowling today, Lovecraft was never a best-selling writer.[5] He wrote in obscurity (by hand), was paid a pittance, and died in genteel poverty. Yet, as Houellebecq points out, "[When] Lovecraft died, his work was born." Since then that work, with Houellebecq's correctly named "great texts" always at the center, has never been out of print, and the books have generated millions and millions of dollars of income.[6]

Yet the *financial* legacy Lovecraft's work is of little concern to Houellebecq and need be of little concern to us. The *creative* legacy, however, should concern us greatly. Houellebecq mentions two writers Lovecraft influenced—Frank Belknap Long and Robert Bloch. There are dozens more, beginning with the Texas prodigy Robert E. Howard, whose stories of Conan the Barbarian are in many cases barely disguised Lovecraft pastiches and gave birth to an entire genre, and perhaps ending with Joyce Carol Oates, who has spoken highly of Lovecraft and acknowledged his influence on at least some of her more gothic work. Between Howard and Oates (and it is difficult for me to imagine a literary gulf much wider) is an entire pantheon of writers who have been touched by Lovecraft and his dreams, sometimes directly, sometimes at second hand (in discovering Robert Bloch at the age of ten, for example, I was inadvertently discovering Lovecraft), sometimes forcefully, sometimes with the barest brush of one outstretched wing of imagina-

---

[5] Few lines have moved me so deeply as the simple sentence which ends Houellebecq's account of HPL's fruitless job-hunting in New York: "And he began to sell his furniture." (p. 97)

[6] Where it went, where it goes now, and where it will continue to go until Lovecraft's work enters the public domain would make an interesting study in and of itself. His brief marriage to Sonia Greene produced no issue, and for many years most of HPL's copyrights were held by Arkham House, a company founded by Donald Wandrei and August Derleth, two writers profoundly influenced by Lovecraft. Derleth and the temperamental Wandrei had a falling out, and Derleth continued to run Arkham House until his death. Many of Lovecraft's copyrights now appear to be owned by April Derleth, August Derleth's daughter. One thing is certain: somewhere, *someone* has made millions from the estate of this lonely genius, who died next door to destitute.

tion. Such a list of writers would include Clark Ashton Smith, William Hope Hodgson, Fritz Leiber, Harlan Ellison, Jonathan Kellerman, Peter Straub, Charles Willeford, Poppy Z. Brite, James Crumley, John D. MacDonald, Michael Chabon, Ramsey Campbell, Kingsley Amis, Neil Gaiman, Flannery O'Connor, and Tennessee Williams. This is just where the list *starts,* mind you.

Nor are these necessarily the important people. For most developing readers, there comes a dangerous "dead spot" between the ages of thirteen and seventeen. It's that time when most young people put down the books of their childhood but before they pick up those of adulthood. As we know, many children never bridge that gap; when they become adults and we go into their homes, we will be apt to find *Reader's Digest,* the *National Enquirer, Jokes for the John,* and not much else. Some children during that passage of years put down Nancy Drew and R. L. Stine in favor of Agatha Christie, Dean Koontz, perhaps Stoker's *Dracula.* They are the ones who will stock their future homes with the current bestsellers of the moment and continue to provide Danielle Steel's retirement portfolio with fresh stocks.

But there is a third group—always a third group—who cannot be satisfied with such pale fare; who feel a need for something more... dangerous. Yes. Even if it speaks to them from inside the pillow late at night, when the moon peering in the window looks like a skull rather than some romantic image out of a pop song. Yes, even so. And I think it's this third group that has kept Lovecraft alive long after his death, and—irony of ironies—in spite of his own adamant stand against life.

All literature, but especially literature of the weird and the fantastic, is a cave where both readers and writers *hide* from life. (Which is exactly why so many parents and teachers, spotting a teenager with a collection of stories by Lovecraft, Bloch, or Clark Ashton Smith, are apt to cry, "Why are you reading *that* useless junk?") It is in just such caves—such places of refuge—that we lick our wounds and prepare for the next battle out in the real world. Our need for such places never subsides, as any reader of escapist literature will tell you, but they are especially valuable for the potentially serious reader—and writer—who is going through those vulnerable years when the evolution from the child's imagination to the more sophisticated and organized adult's imagination is happening. When, in short, the creative imagination is *molting*.[7]

Understand me here. I must leave you in Michel Houellebecq's capable hands, and I would be understood before I go. I am not saying that Lovecraft (or Leiber, or Ashton Smith, or even myself) was an immature writer, best understood by immature minds who can easily discard him once the storms of adolescence have subsided. That's a canard as old as the early, dismissive critiques of Poe. They did poor service to him, and would do poorer service still to Lovecraft, whose "great texts" remain landmarks of imaginative achievement and reward the reader of fifty as richly as the bright child of fifteen. My point (my *final* point, you may be grateful to note) is that Lovecraft's *mature* achievements have never been more splendidly validated than they are by Michel Houellebecq. If you've read all of Lovecraft, *Against the World, Against Life* may tempt you back to him, and cause you to see him in a new light; if you are coming to the Dark Prince of Providence for the first time, you could not have a more invigorating and exciting opener of the way.

And—to quote Robert Bloch—pleasant dreams.

Stephen King
Bangor, Maine
December 10, 2004

---

[7] Or, in too many cases—god*damn* this society—shriveling away to something that can only imagine someday driving a Dodge Hemi or (here's a stretch) having a successful audition for *American Idol.*

H. P. LOVECRAFT CHRONOLOGY

1890 August 20—Howard Phillips Lovecraft is born at 454 (then numbered 194) Angell Street in Providence, Rhode Island.

1897 HPL writes "The Poem of Ulysses," his earliest surviving work.

1906 HPL's first appearance in print: a letter about astronomy to the *Providence Sunday Journal*.

1908 HPL writes "The Alchemist," after which he enters a five-year period of solitude and a drought of productivity.

1913 HPL attacks the "insipid love stories" of writer Fred Jackson in a series of letters to *The Argosy*. One such letter takes the form of a fourty-four-line satire in the manner of Pope's *Dunciad*. As a result, the United Amateur Press Association invites HPL to join their ranks.

1917 HPL writes "The Tomb" and "Dagon."

1919 HPL writes "Beyond the Wall of Sleep," "The Doom that Came to Sarnath," "The Statement of Randolph Carter," "The Transition of Juan Romero," and "The White Ship." November— HPL travels to Boston's Copley Plaza where he attends a reading by Lord Dunsany of *The Queen's Enemies*, providing HPL with his "greatest literary stimulus... since discovering Poe."

1920 HPL completes "The Cats of Ulthar," "Celephaïs," "Nyar-lathotep," and "The Pictures in the House."

1921 HPL writes "The Music of Erich Zann," "Ashes" (with C. M. Eddy, Jr.), "The Nameless City," and "The Outsider." July 4—HPL attends the first Amateur Journalist convention in Boston where he meets Sonia Haft Greene.

1922 HPL writes "Hypnos," "Azathoth," "The Horror at Martin's Beach" (written with Sonia), "The Hound," "Herbert West–Reanimator," "What the Moon Brings," and "The Lurking Fear."

1924 March 3—HPL and Sonia Haft Greene are married. He moves into Sonia's apartment in Brooklyn, where he writes "The Shunned House" and "Under the Pyramids" (with Harry Houdini).

1925 HPL writes "The Horror at Red Hook" and "He."

1926 April 17—HPL writes one of his most famous stories, "The Call of Cthulhu," as well as "Cool Air," "Pickman's Model," "The Dream-Quest of Unknown Kadath," and "The Silver Key."

1927 HPL writes "The Case of Charles Dexter Ward," "History of the Necronomicon," and "The Colour Out of Space."

1928 HPL writes "The Dunwich Horror."

1929 Sonia files for divorce from HPL.

1930 HPL completes "The Whisperer in Darkness."

1931 HPL writes "At the Mountains of Madness" and "The Shadow Over Innsmouth," two more of the "great texts."

1932 HPL writes "The Dreams in the Witch House."

1934 HPL completes "The Shadow Out of Time," the last of his "great texts."

1937 March 10—HPL enters Jane Brown Memorial Hospital after a two-year battle with intestinal cancer. He dies five days later.

H. P. LOVECRAFT

AGAINST THE WORLD,
AGAINST LIFE

PREFACE TO THE SECOND
FRENCH EDITION

When I began this essay (I believe toward the end of 1988) I was in the same boat as some tens of thousands of other readers. Having discovered Lovecraft's stories at the age of sixteen, I had promptly immersed myself in all his works that had been available in French.[1] Later, with lessening interest, I had explored the work of those who continued the myth of Cthulhu, as well as those authors Lovecraft had felt closest to (Dunsany, Robert Howard, Clark Ashton Smith). From time to time, quite often, I would return to Lovecraft's "great texts"; they continued to exert a strange attraction over me that contradicted my other literary tastes—I knew absolutely nothing about his life.

In hindsight, it seems to me I wrote this book as a sort of first novel. A novel with a single character (H. P. Lovecraft himself)—a novel that was constrained in that all the facts it conveyed and all the texts it cited had to be exact, but a sort of novel nonetheless. The first thing that had surprised me when I discovered Lovecraft

---

[1] This, at the time, was quite difficult. The situation has changed completely thanks to the publication of three Lovecraft volumes in the "Bouquins" collection (Robert Laffont) under the direction of Francis Lacassin.

was his absolute materialism; unlike some of his admirers and commentators, he never considered his myths, his theogonies, his "old races" to be anything other than purely imaginary creations. The other great cause of my surprise was his obsessive racism; never in the reading of his descriptions of nightmare creatures could I have divined that their source was to be found in *real* human beings. For the last half-century the analysis of racism in literature has focused on Céline, yet Lovecraft's case is more interesting and more typical. In his writing, intellectual constructs and analyses of decadence play but a very secondary role. As an author of horror fiction (and one of the finest) he brutally takes racism back to its essential and most profound core: *fear*. His own life is an illustration of this. A country gentleman, convinced of the superiority of his Anglo-Saxon origins, he felt only a remote disdain for other races. His stay in New York's underbelly, in its slums, would change all that. The foreign creatures became *competitors,* enemies, who were close by and whose brute strength far surpassed his. It was then, in a progressive delirium of masochism and terror, that came his calls to massacre.

Having said this, the transposition is absolute. In general, few authors, even amongst those most entrenched in fantasy literature, have made *so few* concessions to the real. Speaking for myself, I have obviously not adhered to Lovecraft's hatred of all forms of realism and his appalled rejection of all subjects relating to money or sex; but perhaps, many years later, I did benefit from the lines where I praise him for having "exploded the casing of the traditional narrative" through his systematic use of scientific terms and concepts. Regardless, his originality appears to me to be greater today than ever. I wrote at the time that there was something "not really literary" about Lovecraft's work. This has since been bizarrely confirmed. At book signings, once in a while, young people come to see me and ask me to sign this book. They have discovered Lovecraft through role-playing games or CD-ROMs. They have not read his work and don't even intend to do so. Nonetheless, oddly, they want to find out more—beyond the texts—about the individual and about how he constructed his world.

This extraordinary ability to create a universe, this visionary power, probably struck me too greatly at the time and prevented me—this is my only regret—from paying sufficient homage to Lovecraft's style. His writing, in fact, is not implemented entirely through hypertrophy and delirium; there is also at times a delicacy in his work, a luminous depth that is altogether rare. This is especially true in the case of "The Whisperer in Darkness," a story I had omitted in my essay and in which one finds paragraphs such as this: *"Besides, there was a strangely calming element of cosmic beauty in the hypnotic landscape through which we climbed and plunged fantastically. Time had lost itself in the labyrinths behind, and around us stretched only the flowering waves of faery and the recaptured loveliness of vanished centuries—the hoary groves, the untainted pastures edged with gay autumnal blossoms, and at vast intervals the small brown farmsteads nestling amidst huge trees beneath vertical precipices of fragrant brier and meadow-grass. Even the sunlight assumed a supernal glamour, as if some special atmosphere or exhalation mantled the whole region. I had seen nothing like it before save in the magic vistas that sometimes form the background of Italian primitives. Sodoma and Leonardo conceived such expanses, but only in the distance, and through the vaultings of Renaissance arcades. We were now burrowing bodily through the midst of the picture, and I seemed to find in its necromancy a thing I had innately known or inherited and for which I had always been vainly searching."* [*The Call of Cthulhu and Other Weird Stories*, H. P. Lovecraft, Penguin 1999, p. 243] Here, we are at a point where the extreme acuity of sensory perception is about to propel us into a philosophical perception of the world; in other words, here we are inside poetry.

Michel Houellebecq, 1998

PART ONE

ANOTHER UNIVERSE

"Perhaps one needs to have suffered a great deal in order to appreciate Lovecraft…"
                                                        Jacques Bergier

Life is painful and disappointing. It is useless, therefore, to write new realistic novels. We generally know where we stand in relation to reality and don't care to know any more. Humanity, such as it is, inspires only an attenuated curiosity in us. All those prodigiously refined "notations," "situations," anecdotes… All they do, once a book has been set aside, is reinforce the slight revulsion that is already adequately nourished by any one of our "real life" days.

Now, here is Howard Phillips Lovecraft: *"I am so beastly tired of mankind and the world that nothing can interest me unless it contains a couple of murders on each page or deals with the horrors unnameable and unaccountable that leer down from the external universes."*

Howard Phillips Lovecraft (1890–1937). We need a supreme antidote against all forms of realism.

★ ★ ★

Those who love life do not read. Nor do they go to the movies, actually. No matter what might be said, access to the artistic universe is more or less entirely the preserve of those who are a little *fed up* with the world.

As for Lovecraft, he was more than a little fed up. In 1908 at the age of eighteen, he suffered what has been described as a "nervous breakdown" and plummeted into a lethargy that lasted about ten years. At the age when his old classmates were hurriedly turning their backs on childhood and diving into life as into some marvelous, uncensored adventure, he cloistered himself at home, speaking only to his mother, refusing to get up all day, wandering about in a dressing gown all night.

What's more, he wasn't even writing.

What was he doing? Reading a little, maybe. We can't even be sure of this. In fact, his biographers have had to admit they don't know much at all, and that, judging from appearances—at least between the ages of eighteen and twenty-three—he did absolutely nothing.

Then, between 1913 and 1918, very slowly, the situation improved. Gradually, he reestablished contact with the human race. It was not easy. In May 1918 he wrote to Alfred Galpin: *"I am only about half alive—a large part of my strength is consumed in sitting up or walking. My nervous system is a shattered wreck and I am absolutely bored and listless save when I come upon something which peculiarly interests me."*

It is definitely pointless to embark on a dramatic or psychological reconstruction. Because Lovecraft is a lucid, intelligent, and sincere man. A kind of lethargic terror descended upon him as he turned eighteen years old and he knew the reason for it perfectly well. In a 1920 letter he revisits his childhood at length. The little railway set whose cars were made of packing-cases, the coach house where he had set up his puppet theater. And later, the garden he had designed, laying out each of its paths. It was irrigated by a system of canals that were his own handiwork, its ledges enclosed a small lawn at the center of which stood a sundial. It was, he said, "the paradise of my adolescent years."

Then comes this passage that concludes the letter: *"Then I perceived with horror that I was growing too old for pleasure. Ruthless Time had set its fell claw upon me, and I was seventeen. Big boys do not play in toy houses and mock gardens, so I was obliged to turn over my world in sorrow to another and younger boy who dwelt across the lot from me. And since that time I have not delved in the earth or laid out paths and roads. There is too much wistful memory in such procedure, for the fleeting joy of childhood may never be recaptured. Adulthood is hell."*

Adulthood is hell. In the face of such a trenchant position, "moralists" today will utter vague opprobrious grumblings while waiting for a chance to strike with their obscene intimations. Perhaps Lovecraft actually could not become an adult; what is certain is that he did not want to. And given the values that govern the adult world, how can you argue with him? The reality principle, the pleasure principle, competitiveness, permanent challenges, sex and status—hardly reasons to rejoice.

Lovecraft, for his part, knew he had nothing to do with this world. And at each turn he played a losing hand. In theory and in practice. He lost his childhood; he also lost his faith. The world sickened him and he saw no reason to believe that by *looking at things better* they might appear differently. He saw religions as so many sugar-coated illusions made obsolete by the progress of science. At times, when in an exceptionally good mood, he would speak of the enchanted circle of religious belief, but it was a circle

31

from which he felt banished, anyway.

Few beings have ever been so impregnated, pierced to the core, by the conviction of the absolute futility of human aspiration. The universe is nothing but a furtive arrangement of elementary particles. A figure in transition toward chaos. That is what will finally prevail. The human race will disappear. Other races in turn will appear and disappear. The skies will be glacial and empty, traversed by the feeble light of half-dead stars. These too will disappear. Everything will disappear. And human actions are as free and as stripped of meaning as the unfettered movement of the elementary particles. Good, evil, morality, sentiments? Pure "Victorian fictions." All that exists is egotism. Cold, intact, and radiant.

Lovecraft was well aware of the distinctly depressing nature of his conclusions. As he wrote in 1918, *"all rationalism tends to minimalize the value and the importance of life, and to decrease the sum total of human happiness. In some cases the truth may cause suicidal or nearly suicidal depression."*

He remained steadfast in his materialism and atheism. In letter after letter he returned to his convictions with distinctly masochistic delectation.

Of course, life has no meaning. But neither does death. And this is another thing that curdles the blood when one discovers Lovecraft's universe. The deaths of his heroes have no meaning. Death brings no appeasement. It in no way allows the story to conclude. Implacably, HPL destroys his characters, evoking only the dismemberment of marionettes. Indifferent to these pitiful vicissitudes, cosmic fear continues to expand. It swells and takes form. Great Cthulhu emerges from his slumber.

What is Great Cthulhu? An arrangement of electrons, like us. Lovecraft's terror is rigorously material. But, it is quite possible, given the free interplay of cosmic forces, that Great Cthulhu possesses abilities and powers to act that far exceed ours. Which, *a priori,* is not particularly reassuring at all.

From his journeys to the penumbral worlds of the unutterable, Lovecraft did not return to bring us good news. Perhaps, he confirmed, something is hiding behind the curtain of reality that at times allows itself to be perceived. Something truly vile, in fact.

It is possible, in fact, that beyond the narrow range of our perception, other entities exist. Other creatures, other races, other concepts and other minds. Amongst these entities some are probably far superior to us in intelligence and in knowledge. But this is not necessarily good news. What makes us think that these creatures, different as they are from us, will exhibit any kind of a *spiritual* nature? There is nothing to suggest a transgression of the universal laws of egotism and malice. It is ridiculous to imagine that at the edge of the cosmos, other well-intentioned and wise beings await to guide us toward some sort of harmony. In order to imagine how they might treat us were we to come into contact with them, it might be best to recall how we treat "inferior intelligences" such as rabbits and frogs. In the best of cases they serve as *food* for us; sometimes also, often in fact, we kill them for the sheer pleasure of killing. This, Lovecraft warned, would be the true picture of our future relationship to those other intelligent beings. Perhaps some of the more beautiful human specimens would be honored and would end up on a dissection table—that's all.

And once again, none of it will make any sense.

O humans at the end of the twentieth century, this desolate cosmos is absolutely our own. This abject universe where fear mounts in concentric circles, layer upon layer, until the unnameable is revealed, this universe where our only conceivable destiny is to be *pulverized* and *devoured,* we must recognize it absolutely as being our own mental universe. And for whoever wants to know this collective state of mind through a quick and accurate survey, Lovecraft's success is itself a symptom. Today, more so than ever before, we can utter the *declaration of principles* that begins "Arthur

Jermyn" as our own: *"Life is a hideous thing, and from the background behind what we know of it peer daemoniacal hints of truth which make it sometimes a thousandfold more hideous."*

The paradox, however, is that we prefer this universe, hideous as it is, to our own reality. In this, we are precisely the readers that Lovecraft anticipated. We read his tales with the same exact disposition as that which prompted him to write them. Satan or Nyarlathotep, either one will do, but we will not tolerate another moment of *realism*. And, truth be told, given his prolonged acquaintance with the disgraceful turns of our ordinary sins, the value of Satan's currency has dropped a little. Better Nyarlathotep, ice-cold, evil, and inhuman. *Subb-haqqua Nyarlathotep!*

It's clear why reading Lovecraft is paradoxically comforting to those souls who are weary of life. In fact, it should perhaps be prescribed to all who, for one reason or other, have come to feel a true aversion to life in all its forms. In some cases, the jolt to the nerves upon a first reading is immense. One may find oneself smiling all alone, or humming a tune from a musical. One's outlook on existence is, in a word, modified.

Ever since the virus was first introduced into France by Jacques Bergier, the increase in the number of readers has been substantial. Like most of those contaminated, I myself discovered HPL at sixteen through the intermediary of a "friend." To call it a shock would be an understatement. I had not known literature was capable of this. And, what's more, I'm still not sure it is. There is something not really literary about Lovecraft's work.

To make this case, let us first consider the fact that fifteen or so writers (Belknap Long, Robert Bloch, Lin Carter, Fred Chappell, August Derleth, Donald Wandrei, to name a few…) consecrated all or part of their careers to developing and enriching the myths created by HPL. And not furtively so, nor in hiding, but most avowedly. The filial lineage is even further systematically reinforced by the use of the exact same *words*. These take on the value of incantations (the wild hills west of Arkham, Miskatonic University, the city of Irem with its thousand pillars... R'lyeh, Sarnath, Dagon, Nyarlathotep... and above all the unnameable, the blasphemous *Necronomicon* whose name can only be uttered in a whisper), *lâ! lâ! Shub-Niggurath! The Goat of the Woods with a Thousand Young!*

In an age that exalts originality as a supreme value in the arts, this phenomenon is surely cause for surprise. In fact, as Francis Lacassin opportunely points out, nothing like it has been recorded since Homer and medieval epic poetry. We must humbly acknowledge that we are dealing here with what is known as a "founding mythology."

RITUAL LITERATURE

To create a great popular myth is to create a ritual that the reader awaits impatiently and to which he can return with mounting pleasure, seduced each time by a different repetition of terms, ever so imperceptibly altered to allow him to reach a new depth of experience.

Presented thus, things appear almost simple. And yet, rare are the successes in the history of literature. In reality, it is no easier than creating a new religion.

To clearly understand what is at play, one would have had to personally experience the sense of frustration that invaded England with the death of Sherlock Holmes. Conan Doyle had no choice: he had to resurrect his hero. When, vanquished by death, he in turn laid down arms, the world was engulfed by a sad sense of resignation. We would have to make do with the fifty-odd existing "Sherlock Holmes" stories, reading and rereading them tirelessly. We would have to make do with those who would continue these stories and with commentators; and we would have to greet the inevitable (and at times amusing) parodies with a resigned smile, while all the while in our hearts we nourished the impossible dream that the central core, the very heart of the myth, would continue. An old Indian army trunk would turn up some-where, and magically preserved therein, unpublished "Sherlock Holmes" stories...

Lovecraft, who admired Conan Doyle, succeeded in creating a myth as popular, as lively and irresistible. One might even say that the two men had in common a remarkable *talent for story-telling*. Of course. But there is something else at work. Neither Alexandre Dumas nor Jules Verne were mediocre storytellers. And yet, nothing in their work comes close to the stature of the Baker Street detective.

The Sherlock Holmes stories are centered on a character, whereas in Lovecraft one does not meet any truly human speci-mens. Of course, this is an important distinction; very important, but not truly essential. It can be compared to what separates theist from atheist religions. The fundamental character that brings them together, the so-called *religious* character, is otherwise difficult to define and to broach directly.

Another small difference that might be noted—minimal to lit-erary history, tragic to the individual—is that Conan Doyle had ample occasion to realize that he was creating an essential mytho-logy. Lovecraft did not. At the moment of his death he had the clear impression that his creative work would plunge into ob-scurity along with him.

Nonetheless, he already had disciples. Not that he considered them as such. He did indeed correspond with young writers (Bloch, Belknap Long, and others), but did not necessarily advise them to take the same path as him. He did not present himself as either a master or a model. He greeted their first ventures with exemplary delicacy and modesty. He was courteous, considerate, and kind, a true friend to them, never a teacher.

Absolutely incapable of leaving a letter unanswered, neglecting to request payment when his literary-revision work went unpaid, systematically underestimating his contribution to stories that without him would never have seen the light of day, Lovecraft conducted himself like an authentic *gentleman* throughout his life.

Of course, he liked the idea of becoming a writer. But he was not attached to this *above all else.* In 1925, in a moment of despondency, he writes, *"I am well-nigh resolv'd to write no more tales, but merely to dream when I have a mind to, not stopping to do any thing so vulgar as to set down the dream for a boarish Publick. I have concluded that Literature is no proper pursuit for a gentleman; and that Writing ought never to be consider'd but as an elegant Accomplishment to be indulg'd in with infrequency, and Discrimination."*

Thankfully, he did continue, and his greatest stories were written subsequent to this letter. But until the very end, he remained, above all, as he liked to describe himself, a kind old gentleman from Providence. And never, never a professional writer.

Paradoxically, Lovecraft's character is fascinating in part because his values were so entirely opposite to ours. He was fundamentally racist, openly reactionary, he glorified puritanical inhibitions, and evidently found all "direct erotic manifestations" repulsive. Resolutely anticommercial, he despised money, considered democracy to be an idiocy and progress to be an illusion. The word "freedom," so cherished by Americans, prompted only a sad, derisive guffaw. Throughout his life, he maintained a typically aristocratic, scornful attitude toward humanity in general coupled with extreme kindness toward individuals in particular.

Whatever the case, all those who had dealings with Lovecraft *as an individual* felt an immense sadness when they learned of his death. Robert Bloch said that had he known the truth about the state of his health, he would have dragged himself on his knees all the way to Providence to see him. August Derleth consecrated the rest of his existence to collecting, compiling, and publishing the posthumous fragments of his departed friend.

And, it is thanks to Derleth and a few others (but primarily Derleth) that Lovecraft's body of work has reached the world. Today, it stands before us, an imposing baroque structure, its towering strata rising in so many layered concentric circles, a wide and sumptuous landing around each—the whole surrounding a vortex of pure horror and absolute marvel.

—The first, outermost circle: the correspondence and poems. These are only partially published, and even more partially translated. The correspondence is rather staggering: almost one hundred thousand letters, some of which are thirty or forty pages long. As for the poems, a precise count does not currently exist.

—A second circle would contain those stories Lovecraft participated in, either those conceived of as a collaboration to begin with (like the stories he wrote with Kenneth Sterling or Robert Barlow, for example) or others, whose authors may have benefited from Lovecraft's revisions (there are extremely numerous examples of these; the substance of Lovecraft's collaborations varied and sometimes went as far as a complete rewrite of the text).

To these we may also add the stories written by Derleth based on notes and fragments left behind by Lovecraft.

—With the third circle we come to the stories that were actually written by Howard Phillips Lovecraft. Here, obviously, each word counts; these have all been published in French and we cannot expect their number to ever increase.

—Finally, we can draw a definitive fourth circle, at the absolute heart of HPL's myth, that contains what most rabid Lovecraftians continue to call, almost in spite of themselves, the "great texts." I will cite them here for the pleasure of it alone, along with the date of their composition:

"The Call of Cthulhu" (1926)
"The Colour Out of Space" (1927)
"The Dunwich Horror" (1928)
"The Whisperer in Darkness" (1930)
"At the Mountains of Madness" (1931)
"The Dreams in the Witch House" (1932)
"The Shadow Over Innsmouth" (1932)
"The Shadow Out of Time" (1934)

Moreover, suspended above HPL's entire edifice, like a thick unstable fog, is the strange shadow of his own personality. One might find the cultlike atmosphere surrounding his character, his actions and movements, and even his most insignificant pieces of writing somewhat exaggerated or even morbid. But I guarantee that opinion is bound to be revised quickly after a plunge into the "great texts." It's only natural to initiate a cult to one who proffers such benefits.

Successive generations of Lovecraftians have done just this. As is always the case, the "recluse of Providence" has now become almost as mythic a figure as one of his own creations. And what is most startling is that all attempts at demystification have *failed*. No degree of biographical detail has succeeded in dissipating the aura of strange pathos that surrounds the character. And five hundred pages into his book, Sprague de Camp is forced to admit: "I do not pretend to completely understand H. P. Lovecraft." No matter who one imagines him to have been, Howard Phillips Lovecraft was truly a *very* unique human being.

Lovecraft's body of work can be compared to a gigantic dream machine, of astounding breadth and efficacy. There is nothing tranquil or discreet in his literature. Its impact on the reader's mind is savagely, frighteningly brutal, and dangerously slow to dissipate. Rereading produces no notable modification other than that, eventually, one ends up wondering: *how does he do it?*

In the specific case of HPL there is nothing ridiculous or offensive about such a question. In fact, what characterizes his work compared to a "normal" work of literature, is that his disciples feel they can, at least theoretically, through the judicious use of the same ingredients as those indicated by the master, obtain results of an equal or higher quality.

No one has ever seriously envisioned *continuing* Proust. Lovecraft, they have. And it's not a matter of secondary works presented as homage, nor of parodies, but truly a continuation. Which is unique in the history of modern literature.

What's more, the role HPL plays as the *generator of dreams* is not limited to literature alone. His work, at least to the same extent as R. E. Howard's, although often less obviously, has been a profound factor in the renaissance of fantasy illustration. Even rock music, usually so distrustful of all things literary, has made a point of paying homage to him—an homage, one might say, paid by one great power to another, by one mythology to another. As for the implications of Lovecraft's writing in the domains of architecture or film, they will be immediately apparent to the sensitive reader. This is the building of a new world.

Hence the importance of building blocks and of construction techniques. To prolong the impact.

PART TWO

TECHNICAL ASSAULT

The surface of the planet today is covered in a chain-linked mesh of associations that join together to form a man-made network of irregular density.

Through this network, society's lifeblood circulates. The transport of people, of merchandise, of commodities; multiple transactions, sales orders, purchase orders, bits of information, all pass each other by; there are also other, more strictly intellectual or affective exchanges that occur. This incessant flux bewilders humanity, engrossed as it tends to be by the cadaverous leaps and bounds of its own activities.

But, in a few spots where the network's links are weakly woven, strange entities may allow a seeker, one who "thirsts for knowledge," to discern their existence. In every place where human activity is interrupted, where there is *a blank on the map*, these ancient gods crouch huddled waiting to take back their rightful place.

As in the terrifying interior Arabian desert, the Rub-al-Khalid, from whence a Mohammedan poet named Abdul Al-Hazred was returning around 731 after ten years of utter solitude.

Having grown indifferent to the practices of Islam, he consecrated the years that followed to writing an impious and blasphemous book, the repugnant *Necronomicon* (several copies of which escaped the pyre and traversed the ages) before being devoured by invisible monsters in broad daylight at the Damascus market square.

As in the unexplored plains of Northern Tibet, where degenerate Tcho-Tchos lope around in adoration of unnameable deities they qualify as "the Great Old Ones."

And as in the huge expanses of the South Pacific, where the paradoxical trails of unexpected volcanic convulsions at times produce utterly inhuman sculptures and geometry which the abject and depraved natives of the Tuamotu archipelago worship, crawling forward on their upper bodies.

At the intersections of these channels of communication, man has erected giant ugly metropolises where each person, isolated in an anonymous apartment, in a building identical to the others, believes absolutely that he is the center of the world and the measure of all things. But beneath the warrens of these burrowing insects, very ancient and very powerful creatures are slowly awakening from their slumber. During the Carboniferous age, during the Triassic and the Permian ages, they were here already; they have heard the roars of the very first mammals and will know the howls of agony of the very last.

Howard Phillips Lovecraft was not a theoretician. Jacques Bergier clearly understood that, by introducing materialism into the heart of fear and fantasy, HPL created a new genre. It is no longer a question of believing or not believing, as in certain vampire or werewolf tales; there is no possible reinterpretation, there is no escape. There exists no horror less psychological, less *debatable*.

Nonetheless, he seems not to have been fully conscious of what he was doing. Although he actually consecrated a one-hundred-and-fifty-page essay to the subject of horror literature, in reading it over, "Supernatural Horror in Literature" is a little disappointing; frankly, it even feels mildly *dated*. And we finally understand why: it is simply because it does not take Lovecraft's own contribution to the genre into account. We learn a lot about the wide range of his culture and about his tastes. We learn that he admired Poe, Dunsany, Machen, and Blackwood: but nothing in it portends what he would write himself.

The essay was written around 1925–1926, hence immediately before HPL embarked on writing the "great texts" series. This is probably not sheer coincidence; although not consciously, and perhaps not even unconsciously, one would almost tend to say *organically,* Lovecraft must have felt a need to recapitulate all that had been done in the domain of horror fiction before exploding its casing and setting off on radically new paths.

In the quest for the compositional techniques used by HPL, we might also be tempted to look for clues in his letters, commentaries, and the advice he gave his young correspondents. But here too, the result is disconcerting and disappointing. In the first place because Lovecraft takes his correspondent's personality into account. He always begins by trying to understand what it was the author had set out to do and only then does he formulate precise and punctual advice adapted exactly to the story he is writing about. What's more, he frequently gives recommendations that he himself seems to be the first to disobey, such as "must not overuse adjectives such as monstrous, unnameable, and unmentionable." Which, given his own work, is rather surprising. The only point of any general application is to be found in a letter to Frank Belknap Long: *"The one thing I never do is sit down and seize a pen with the deliberate intention of writing a story. Nothing but hack work ever comes of that. The only stories I write are those whose central ideas, pictures, and moods occur to me spontaneously."*

Still, Lovecraft is not entirely indifferent to the question of *compositional technique*. Like Baudelaire and Edgar Poe, he is fascinated by the idea that through the rigid application of certain schemas, certain formulas, certain symmetries, perfection may be accessed. And he even attempts a first conceptualization in the small thirty-page manuscript entitled *The Commonplace Book*.

In its very brief first section he gives general advice on how to write a story (weird or not). He then attempts to establish a typology of "certain basic underlying horrors effectively used in weird fiction." As for the book's last section, by far its longest, it consists of a series of staggered notes made between 1919 and 1935 that for the most part consist of a single sentence and each of which could serve as the starting point for a weird tale.

With his habitual generosity, Lovecraft was happy to lend out this manuscript to friends, telling them to feel free to use any of the ideas in it to create a vintage brew all their own.

In fact, above all, this *Commonplace Book* is a surprising stimulant for the imagination. It contains the seeds of dizzying ideas, nine-tenths of which were never developed by Lovecraft nor by others. And its all too short theoretical section conveys Lovecraft's high regard for horror literature, his belief in its absolute generality and its close link to the fundamental elements of human consciousness (as a "basic element of horror," for example, he cites "Any mysterious and irresistible march toward a doom").

But where techniques of composition used by HPL are concerned, we haven't made any more headway. If the *Commonplace Book* furnishes the building blocks, it gives us no indication of how to assemble them. And perhaps it is asking too much of Lovecraft. It is difficult and may even be impossible to possess his level of genius and, at the same time, to be aware of that genius.

There is only one way to try to find out more. Besides, it's the most logical way: to immerse oneself in the texts, the fiction written by HPL. First the "great texts," those written in the last ten years of his life when he was at the height of his capacities. But also anterior texts; where we can see the methods of his art coming to life one by one, like musical instruments, each attempting a fleeting solo before plunging together into the fury of a demented opera.

ATTACK THE STORY
LIKE A RADIANT SUICIDE

A classic understanding of the weird story might be summarized as follows. At first nothing at all happens. The characters are bathed in banal and beatific happiness, adequately symbolized by the family life of an insurance agent in an American suburb. The kids play baseball, the woman plays piano a little, etc. All is well.

Then, gradually, almost insignificant incidents accumulate, dangerously reinforcing one another. Cracks appear in the glossy varnish of the ordinary, leaving the field wide open for troublesome hypotheses. Inexorably, the forces of evil enter the setting.

It must be noted that this approach has produced some truly impressive results. As high points, one can cite the tales of Richard Matheson, who at the peak of his art clearly enjoyed choosing utterly banal settings (supermarkets, gas stations…) and intentionally describing them in a dull and prosaic manner.

Howard Phillips Lovecraft's approach was entirely opposite. For him there were no "cracks in the glossy varnish of the ordinary," no "almost insignificant incidents." None of that interested him. He had no wish to spend thirty or even three pages describing an average American family. He was, in fact, willing to document just about anything else, Aztec rituals or the anatomy of batrachians, but certainly not daily life.

To shed light on the question, let us look at the first few paragraphs of one of the most insidious of Matheson's successes, *Button, Button*:

"The package was lying by the front door—a cube-shaped carton sealed with tape, the name and address printed by hand: MR. AND MRS. ARTHUR LEWIS, 217 E. 37TH STREET, NEW YORK, NEW YORK, 10016. Norma picked it up, unlocked the door and went into the apartment. It was just getting dark.

After she put the lamb chops in the broiler, she made herself a drink and sat down to open the package.

Inside the carton was a push-button unit fastened to a small wooden box. A glass dome covered the button. Norma tried to lift it off, but it was locked in place. She turned the unit over and saw a folded piece of paper Scotch-taped to the bottom of the box. She pulled it off. 'Mr. Steward will call on you at eight p.m.'"

Here now is the assault that opens "The Call of Cthulhu," the first of Lovecraft's "great texts":

The most merciful thing in the world, I think, is the inability of the human mind to correlate all its contents. We live on a placid island of ignorance in the midst of black seas of infinity, and it was not meant that we should voyage far. The sciences, each straining in its own direction, have hitherto harmed us little; but some day the piecing together of dissociated knowledge will open up such terrifying vistas of reality, and of our frightful position therein, that we shall either go mad from the revelation or flee from the deadly light into the peace and safety of a new dark age.

The very least that can be said is that Lovecraft sets the stage. At first glance, this is actually an inconvenience. For indeed it is true that few readers, fans of weird fiction or not, are able to set down Matheson's story without finding out what happens to the godforsaken button. HPL, on the other hand, tends to pick his readers from the start. He writes for an audience of fanatics—readers he was to finally find only years after his death.

In a more hidden and profound way, however, there is a short-coming in the methodology of the horror story that is too slow to start. It only becomes apparent after reading several works written in the same vein. As the ambiguous, rather than terrifying, incidents multiply, the reader's imagination is titillated but never truly fulfilled. It is propelled into motion. And it is always dangerous to leave the reader's imagination at liberty, because left alone, it can reach some atrocious conclusions. And when, after fifty laborious pages, the author finally divulges the secret of his ultimate horror, the reader might feel a little disappointed. He had been expecting something more terrifying.

In his greatest successes, Matheson is able to ward off this danger by introducing a philosophical or moral dimension in the last pages that is so obvious, so poignant and pertinent, that the whole story is suddenly bathed in a different and mortally affecting light. Still, it is his somewhat shorter texts that remain his most beautiful.

As for Lovecraft, he navigates a fifty- or sixty-page or even longer story with ease. At the height of his artistic abilities he needed a space vast enough to contain all the elements of his grandiose machinery. The paroxysmal planes that form the architecture of the "great texts" could hardly be satisfied by a mere ten pages. And *The Case of Charles Dexter Ward* is in fact a short novel.

As for the "fall" so cherished by Americans, for the most part, he is not very interested in it. None of Lovecraft's stories are introverted. Each is an open slice of howling fear. The next story picks the reader's fear up at exactly the same point and nourishes it some more. The great Cthulhu is indestructible, even if peril has been temporarily thwarted. In his home of R'lyeh under the waters he will again begin to wait, to sleep and to dream:

"That is not dead which can eternal lie,
And with strange aeons even death may die"

True to form, it is with disconcerting energy that Lovecraft mounts what could be termed a *massive attack*. And he also feels a predilection for the variant, that is, the theoretical attack. We cite the opening of "Arthur Jermyn" and of "The Call of Cthulhu." These are but so many radiant variations on a single theme: "Abandon all hope, ye who enter here." Let us recall once again the justly celebrated opening of "Beyond the Wall of Sleep":

"I have often wondered if the majority of mankind ever pause to reflect upon the occasionally titanic significance of dreams, and of the obscure world to which they belong. Whilst the greater number of our nocturnal visions are perhaps no more than faint and fantastic reflections of our waking experiences—Freud to the contrary with his puerile symbolism—there are still a certain remainder whose immundane and ethereal character permit of no ordinary interpretation, and whose vaguely exciting and disquieting effect suggests possible minute glimpses into a sphere of mental existence no less important than physical life, yet separated from that life by an all but impassable barrier."

At times he seems to have preferred force to a harmonious arrangement of sentences, as in "The Thing on the Doorstep," whose opening sentence is: *"It is true that I have sent six bullets through the head of my best friend, and yet I hope to show by this statement that I am not his murderer."* But he always chooses style over banality. And the breadth of his methods continues to expand. This is how his 1919 story "The Transition of Juan Romero" begins: *"Of the events which took place at the Norton Mine on October eighteenth and nineteenth, 1894, I have no desire to speak."*

Although it is still a touch dull and prosaic, this attack, nevertheless, heralds the splendid explosion that begins "The Shadow Out of Time," the last of the "great texts," written in 1934:

"After twenty-two years of nightmare and terror, saved only by a desperate conviction of the mythical source of certain impressions, I am unwill-

ing to vouch for the truth of that which I think I found in Western Australia on the night of 17–18 July 1935. There is reason to hope that my experience was wholly or partly an hallucination—for which, indeed, abundant causes existed. And yet, its realism was so hideous that I sometimes find hope impossible."

What is astonishing is that after this opening he is able to maintain the narrative on an ever-increasing level of exaltation. But then, even his greatest detractors agree and concede that he had a somewhat extraordinary imagination.

His characters, on the other hand, do not withstand the assault. And this is the only real shortcoming of his method of massive attack. Often when reading his stories, one wonders why the protagonists are taking so long to understand the nature of the horror menacing them. They appear, frankly, obtuse. And therein lies a real problem. Because if they were to have understood what was going on, no power could prevent them from fleeing, in the grips of the most abject terror. Which event must not occur till the very end of the story.

Did Lovecraft have a solution? Maybe. One can imagine that his characters, while fully aware of the hideous reality to be confronted, choose nonetheless to do so. Such virile courage was decidedly too foreign to Lovecraft's own temperament for him to undertake describing it. Graham Masterton and Lin Carter took steps in this direction; the results, admittedly, are unconvincing. Nonetheless it seems conceivable. We can dream of a mysterious adventure novel whose heroes have the mettle, sturdiness, and tenacity of John Buchan characters as they confront the terrifying and marvelous universe of Howard Phillips Lovecraft.

UTTER THE GREAT NO
TO LIFE WITHOUT WEAKNESS

A bsolute hatred of the world in general, aggravated by an aversion to the modern world in particular. This summarizes Lovecraft's attitude fairly accurately.

Many authors have dedicated their work to elaborating the reasons for this legitimate aversion. Not Lovecraft. For him, hatred of life precedes all literature. He was to remain steadfast in this regard. The rejection of all forms of realism is a preliminary condition for entering his universe.

If an author were to be defined, not by the themes he addresses, but by those he avoids, then we would be forced to agree that Lovecraft's position is rather unique. In his entire body of work, there is not a single allusion to two of the realities to which we generally ascribe great importance: sex and money. Truly not one reference. He writes exactly as though these things did not exist. So much so, that when a female character does intervene in a story (which occurs altogether twice) one feels an odd twinge of bizarreness, as if he had suddenly decided to describe a Japanese person.

In the face of such a radical exclusion, certain critics have concluded that his entire body of work is in fact full of particularly smoldering sexual symbols. Other individuals of a similar intellectual caliber have proffered the diagnosis of "latent homosexuality." Which is supported by nothing in either his correspondence or his life. Yet another useless hypothesis.

In a letter to the young Belknap Long, Lovecraft expresses his thoughts on these questions very distinctly; regarding Fielding's *Tom Jones* that he considers (alas, rightly so) to be the summit of realism, that is to say, of mediocrity:

"In a word, Child, I look upon this sort of writing as a mere prying survey of the lowest part of life, and a slavish transcript of simple events made with the crude feelings of a porter or bargeman [and without any native genius or colour of the creative imagination whatever...] 'Fore God, we can see beasts enough in any barnyard and observe all the mysteries of sex in the breeding of calves and colts. When I contemplate man, I wish to contemplate those characteristicks that elevate him to an human state, and those adornments which lend to his actions the symmetry of creative beauty. 'Tis not that I wish false pompous thoughts and motives imputed to him in the Victorian manner, but that I wish his composition justly apprais'd, with stress lay'd upon those qualities which are peculiarly his, and without the silly praise of such beastly things as he holds in common with any hog or stray goat."

He ends this long diatribe with the following irrefutable principle: *"I do not think that any realism is beautiful."* What we are evidently dealing with is not self-censorship provoked by hidden psychological motives, but an aesthetic conception cleary articulated. This was an important point to establish. Now let's move on.

If Lovecraft frequently reiterates his hostility to all forms of eroticism in art it is because his correspondents (mostly young people, often adolescents even) repeatedly ask him about it. Is it truly certain that erotic or pornographic descriptions can be of no literary interest? Each time he reexamines the question with much good will, but his response never varies: of no interest whatsoever.

As far as he himself was concerned, he had, by age eight, acquired a complete understanding of the subject, thanks to his perusal of an uncle's medical texts. He then explains, "... *after which curiosity was of course impossible. The entire subject had become merely a tedious detail of animal biology, without interest for one whose tastes led him to faery gardens and golden cities glorified by exotick sunsets.*"

It may be tempting not to take this declaration seriously, or to suspect some kind of obscure underlying moral reticence in Lovecraft's attitude. This would be a mistake. Lovecraft was perfectly aware of what puritanical inhibitions were. He adhered to them and occasionally glorified them. But he did so on a different plane that he always distinguished from the plane of pure artistic creation. His views on the subject were complex and precise. And if he refused all sexual allusions in his work, it was first and foremost because he felt such allusions had no place in his aesthetic universe.

On this point, at least, posterity has proven him to be amply justified. There are indeed those who have tried to introduce erotic elements into the framework of a primarily Lovecraftian tale. The results have been absolute failures. Colin Wilson's attempts in particular tend clearly toward catastrophe; there is a constant feeling that the titillating elements have been added merely to draw in a few additional readers. And in truth it cannot be otherwise. The combination is intrinsically impossible.

HPL's writings have but one aim: to bring the reader to a state of *fascination*. The only human sentiments he is interested in are wonderment and fear. He constructs his universe upon these and these alone. It is clearly a limitation, but a conscious, deliberate one. And authentic creativity cannot exist without a certain degree of self-imposed blindness.

★ ★ ★

To understand the origins of Lovecraft's anti-eroticism, it is perhaps fitting to recall that his era was characterized by a desire to be set free from the constraint of "Victorian prudishness." It was during these years, 1920–1930, that stringing a few obscenities together began to be seen as proof of an authentically creative imagination. Lovecraft's young correspondents were naturally marked by this, which is why they persistently questioned him on the subject. And for his part, he answered. With sincerity.

At the time Lovecraft was writing, displaying a variety of sexual experiences was beginning to be considered of interest; in other words, tackling the subject "openly and forthrightly." Such a frank and disengaged attitude did not yet prevail, however, where matters of money, trading transactions, and wealth-management were concerned. It was still customary, when these subjects were brought up, to approach them from a sociological or moral perspective. It was not until the 1960s that true liberation in these matters came about. This is probably why none of his correspondents saw fit to question Lovecraft on this point; money, much like sex, plays no part at all in his stories. There is not the slightest allusion to the financial standing of his characters. This too is of no interest to him whatsoever.

Under such circumstances it is unsurprising that Lovecraft felt no sympathy for the psychologist of the capitalist era, Freud. There was nothing that could seduce him in the "transactional" universe of "transferences" that made you feel you had accidentally stumbled into a business meeting.

But apart from this aversion to psychoanalysis, which actually is common to many artists, Lovecraft had several additional minor reasons to rail against the "Viennese charlatan." It turns out, in fact, that Freud took the liberty of addressing the subject of dreams, and not just once. Dreams were what Lovecraft knew well—they were, in a sense, his preserve. Few writers have used their dreams as systematically as he did; he classified the furnished material, he treated it, at times he was enthusiastic and wrote down a story in the immediate aftermath of a dream without even completely waking (this was true of "Nyarlathotep"), other times he retained certain elements to insert into a new framework; but in any event, he took dreams very seriously.

So, Lovecraft's comportment toward Freud can actually be considered rather mild—he only insulted him two or three times in the course of all his correspondence—but he felt there was only so much to be said, and that the psychoanalytic phenomenon would crumble on its own. Nonetheless, he found time to summarize the fundamentals of Freudian theory in two words: "puerile symbolism." Hundreds of pages may be written on the subject without substantially improving upon this analysis.

Lovecraft didn't really have a novelist's attitude. Most novelists consider it their duty to present an exhaustive picture of life; their mission, to throw a new "light" on it, but where the facts themselves are concerned, they cannot exercise absolute choice. Sex, money, religion, technology, ideology, the distribution of wealth... a good novelist must not ignore any of these. And everything must take place inside a *more or less* coherent rendition of the world. Such a task, is of course, humanly impossible, and the outcome is almost always disappointing. Tough line of work!

Obscurely and unpleasantly, there is also the fact that a novelist tackling the subject of life in general will necessarily discover himself to be more or less compromised by it. This was not a problem Lovecraft experienced. One might well object that the very realities, "animal biology," that so bored him play an integral part in human existence, and that they in fact let the species survive. But he could not have cared less about the survival of the species. "Why worry so much about the future of a doomed world?" was

Oppenheimer's reply to a journalist asking him about the long-term consequences of technological progress.

Uninterested as he was in creating a coherent or acceptable picture of the world, Lovecraft had no reason to make any concessions to life, to phantoms, or to netherworlds. Nor to anyone at all. He deliberately chose to ignore what he considered uninteresting or artistically inferior. And this very limitation gives him power and distinction.

This bias toward *creative limitation,* to reiterate, had nothing to do with any sort of traffic in ideology. When Lovecraft expressed his scorn for "Victorian fictions," for edifying novels that attributed false or pompous motivations to human actions, he was being perfectly sincere. Nor would Sade have found any greater favor in his eyes. His work too is a kind of traffic in ideology. An attempt to make reality fit a prefabricated schema. Nonsense! Lovecraft does not try to repaint the elements of reality that displease him; he resolutely ignores them.

He justified his position quickly in a letter: *"In art there is no use in heeding the chaos of the universe; for so complete is this chaos, that no piece writ in words cou'd even so much as hint at it. I can conceive of no true image of the pattern of life and cosmic force, unless it be a jumble of mean dots arrang'd in directionless spirals."*

But Lovecraft's point of view cannot be fully understood if the self-imposed limitation is simply seen as a philosophical bias without the understanding that it is also a *technical imperative.* In fact, there are forms of human motivation that do not belong in his work; one of the first choices architects make is what materials to use.

THEN YOU WILL SEE
A MAGNIFICENT CATHEDRAL

A traditional novel may be usefully compared to an old air chamber deflating after being placed in an ocean. A generalized and rather weak flow of air like a trickle of pus ends in arbitrary and indistinct nothingness.

Lovecraft, by contrast, places his hand forcefully on certain parts of the air chamber (sex, money…) from which he wishes to see nothing escape. This is a technique of *constriction*. The result, in the areas he chooses, is a powerful gush, an extraordinary efflorescence of images.

When first reading Lovecraft's stories, the architectural descriptions in "The Shadow Out of Time" and in "At the Mountains of Madness" make a profound impression. Here more so than elsewhere, we find ourselves before a new world. Fear itself disappears. All human sentiments disappear save fascination, never before so purely isolated.

Nonetheless, in the foundations of the gigantic citadels conjured by HPL lie hidden nightmare beings. We know this, but tend to forget it, not unlike his heroes who walk toward their catastrophic destiny as in a dream, carried forth by aesthetic exaltation alone.

Reading these descriptions is at first stimulating, but then discourages any attempt at visual adaptation (pictorial or cinematographic). Images graze the consciousness but none appear sufficiently sublime, sufficiently fantastic; none come close to the pinnacle of dreams. As for actual architectural adaptations, none have as yet been undertaken.

It would not be rash to imagine a young man emerging enthusiastically from a reading of Lovecraft's tales and deciding to pursue a study of architecture. Failure and disappointment would lie in wait. The insipid and dull functionality of modern architecture, its zeal to use simple, meager forms and cold, haphazard materials, are too distinctive to be a product of chance. And no one, at least not for generations to come, will rebuild the faerie lace of the palace of Irem.

One discovers architecture progressively and from a variety of angles, *one moves within it;* this is an element that can never be reproduced in a painting nor even in a film; it is an element Howard Phillips Lovecraft's stories successfully reproduced in somewhat stupefying fashion.

An architect by nature, Lovecraft was not much of a painter; his colors are not really colors; rather, they are moods, or to be exact, *lighting,* whose only function is to offset the architecture he describes. He has a particular predilection for the pallid light of a gibbous, waning moon; but he is also partial to the bloody explosion of a crimson romantic sunset or the limpid crystalline of inaccessible azures.

The demented Cyclopean structures envisioned by HPL shock the spirit violently and definitively, more so even than (and this is paradoxical) the magnificent architectural drawings of Piranesi or Monsu Desiderio. We feel we have already visited these gigantic cities in our dreams. In fact, Lovecraft is only transcribing his own dreams as faithfully as he can. Later on, when looking at a particularly grand architectural monument we find ourselves thinking "this is rather *Lovecraftian*."

The first of the reasons for the writer's success becomes apparent immediately upon perusing his correspondence. Howard Phillips Lovecraft was amongst those few men who experience a violent trancelike state when they look at beautiful architecture. His descriptions of sunrise on the venerable steeples of Providence or the crazy alleys of Marblehead are hyperbolic. Adjectives and exclamations accumulate, he recalls incantatory fragments, his chest swells with enthusiasm as images pile one upon another in his mind; he plunges into a true delirium of ecstasy.

Describing his first impressions of New York to his aunt, he claims he almost fainted with "aesthetic exaltation."

Similarly, when he first looked upon the ridged rooftops of Salem, he saw looming processions of puritans in black robes, with stern faces and strange conical hats who were dragging a howling old woman to the pyre.

Throughout his life Lovecraft dreamed of traveling to Europe; it was something he was never able to do. And yet, if there was one man in America born to appreciate the architectural treasures of the Old World, it was him. When he wrote "faint[ing] with aesthetic exaltation" he was not exaggerating. And it was in all seriousness that he told Kleiner that a man is like a coral insect—that his only destiny is to *"build vast beautiful, mineral things for the moon to delight in after he is dead."*

For want of money, Lovecraft never left America—he barely left New England. But, given the intensity of his reactions upon first seeing Kingsport or Marblehead one can only wonder what he would have felt had he been transported to Salamanca or to Notre-Dame of Chartres.

For, like the great gothic or baroque cathedrals, the dream architecture he describes is a *total* architecture. In it, the heroic harmony of planes and volumes can be experienced viscerally; but in contrast to the gigantic, smooth, bare stone surfaces, are the bell towers, the minarets, the bridges overhanging chasms wrought with ornate exuberance. Bas-reliefs, haut-reliefs and frescos decorate the titanic vaults that lead from one inclined plane to another inclined plane deep in the earth's entrails. Many delineate the grandeur and decadence of an entire race, others that are simpler and more geometric seem to suggest disquieting mystical notions.

H. P. Lovecraft's architecture, like that of great cathedrals, like that of Hindu temples, is much more than a three-dimensional mathematical puzzle. It is entirely imbued with an essential dramaturgy that gives its meaning to the edifice. That dramatizes the very smallest spaces, that uses the conjoint resources of the various plastic arts, that annexes the magic play of light to its own ends. It is *living* architecture because at its foundation lies a living and emotional concept of the world. In other words, it is sacred architecture.

AND YOUR SENSES, VECTORS
OF UNUTTERABLE DERANGEMENT

"The air of death and desertion was ghoulish, and the smell of fish almost insufferable…"

The world stinks. The stench of cadavers and of fish blends together. A sense of failure, a hideous degeneration. The world stinks. There are no ghosts under the tumescent moon; there are only bloated cadavers, swollen and black, about to explode in pestilential vomiting.

As for the sense of touch. To touch other beings, other living entities, is an impious, repugnant experience. Their skin bloated with blisters that ooze putrid pus. Their sucking tentacles, their clutching and chewing appendages, all constitute a constant menace. Beings and their hideous corporeal vigor. A simmering, stinking Nemesis of semi-aborted chimeras, amorphous and nauseating: a sacrilege.

Sight at times delivers terror, but can also transport us before wondrous faeric architecture. But, alas, we do have five senses. And the others converge to prove that the universe is something decidedly *disgusting*.

* * *

It has often been noted that Lovecraft's characters, who, especially in the "great texts," are almost indistinguishable from one another, are merely so many projections of Lovecraft himself. Indeed—only so long as we confine the word "projection" to its simplest meaning. They are projections of the true personality of Lovecraft in much the same way that a plane surface can be the orthogonal projection of a volume. True, the general form is distinct. Usually students or professors at a New England university (preferably, Miskatonic University) who specialize in anthropology or folklore, or sometimes in political economy or in non-Euclidean geometry; discreet and reserved by nature, with long emaciated faces and who by profession and temperament lean more toward the satisfactions of the mind. This is a sort of outline, a *robotic-portrait*; and for the most part it is all we will ever know.

In the beginning Lovecraft did not choose to portray interchangeable *flat* characters. In the stories of his youth he seems to have made an effort each time to depict a different narrator, with a social milieu, a personal story, and even a psychological profile. At times this narrator was a poet or a man animated by *poetic sentiment*; this vein actually produced HPL's most indisputable flops.

Only progressively did he come to see the futility of all psychological differentiation. His characters no longer required it; all they needed was functional sensory equipment. Their sole function, in fact, would be to *perceive*.

It might even be said that the deliberate banality of his characters contributes to reinforcing the compelling nature of Lovecraft's universe. A more obtrusive psychological brushstroke would have only detracted from their testimony and diminished its transparency; we would have left the domain of material horror to enter that of psychological horror. And Lovecraft did not wish to describe psychoses, but repugnant realities.

Nonetheless, his heroes succumb to the stylistic device so

cherished by horror writers that consists of the claim that their story might simply be a nightmare, bred by an overly inflamed imagination due after the reading of impious books. That's fine; we don't believe it for an instant.

Assailed by abominable perceptions, Lovecraft's characters function as silent, motionless, utterly powerless, paralyzed observers. They would like nothing more than to escape, or to plumb the deep torpor of a merciful faint. No such luck. They will remain glued in place while around them the nightmare begins to unravel. While visual, auditory, olfactory, and tactile perceptions accumulate and are deployed in a hideous crescendo.

Lovecraft's literature gives precise and alarming meaning to the celebrated dictum, "a deliberate disordering of all the senses." Few individuals will, for example, find the iodized smell of the sea to be repugnant and foul; few, save of course those who have read "The Shadow Over Innsmouth"; likewise, it's hard to think of a batrachian with any degree of calm after reading HPL. All this makes an intensive reading of his work something of an ordeal.

To transform perceptions of ordinary life into an infinite source of nightmares is the wild hope of every writer of weird fiction. Lovecraft succeeds magnificently by injecting all his descriptions with a unique dash of degenerate drooling. When we set aside his stories we may leave behind the half-caste, semi-amorphous cretinous beings that populate them, the humanoids with their flopping, loping gait, their scaly, rough skin, flat, dilated nostrils and stertorous breathing; sooner or later they shall reenter our lives.

In Lovecraft's universe auditory perception merits a place all its own; HPL did not much care for music and his tastes veered rather toward Gilbert and Sullivan musicals. But in his stories he demonstrates a particularly fine-tuned ear; when a character sitting across from you places his hands on the table and emits a weak sucking noise, or when in another character's laugh you discern the nuance of a *cackle,* or bizarre insect stridulation, you know you are inside a Lovecraftian story. The maniacal precision with which HPL organizes the *soundtrack* to his tales certainly plays an important part in the success of the most frightening of them. I don't mean to allude only to "The Music of Erich Zann," where, exceptionally, it is music alone that provokes cosmic horror; but to all the others where, by subtly alternating visual and auditory perceptions, by at times bringing them together, and then by a sudden, bizarre divergence, he brings us to a definite pitch of abject anxiety.

Here, for example, is a description extracted from "Under the Pyramids," a minor tale he ghostwrote for the magician Harry Houdini, that nonetheless contains some of Howard Phillips Lovecraft's most beautiful verbal extravagances:

"... *suddenly my attention was captured by the realization of something which must have been impinging on my subconscious hearing long before the conscious sense was aware of it. From some still lower chasm in earth's bowels were proceeding certain sounds measure and definite, and like nothing I had ever heard before. That they were very ancient and distinctly ceremonial, I felt almost intuitively; and much reading in Egyptology led me to associate them with the flute, the sambuke, the sistrum, and the tympanum. In their rhythmic piping, droning, rattling and beating I felt an element of terror beyond all the known terrors of earth—a terror peculiarly dissociated from personal fear, and taking the form of a sort of objective pity for our planet, that it should hold within its depths such horrors as must lie beyond these aegipanic cacophonies. The sounds increased in volume, and I felt that they were approaching. Then—and may all the gods of all pantheons unite to keep the like from my ears again—I began to hear, faintly and afar off, the morbid and millennial tramping of the marching things.*

It was hideous that footfalls so dissimilar should move in such perfect rhythm. The training of unhallowed thousands of years must lie behind that march of earth's inmost monstrosities... Padding, clicking, walking, stalking, rumbling, lumbering, crawling... and all to the abhorrent discords of those mocking instruments. And then...

The passage is not a paroxysm. At this stage in the story nothing has really happened. These clicking, crawling, rumbling things will come closer still. You will, finally, *see* them. *"Later, at night, at the hour when everything sleeps, you will likely hear the morbid and millennial tramping of the marching things."* This shouldn't surprise you. It was the plan all along.

WILL MAP OUT
AN INTEGRAL DELIRIUM

"**F**ive slightly longer reddish tubes start from inner angles of starfish-shaped head and end in sac-like swellings of same colour which upon pressure open to bell-shaped orifices 2 inches maximum diameter and lined with sharp white tooth-like projections. Probable mouths. All these tubes, cilia, and points of starfish-head, found folded tightly down; tubes and points clinging to bulbous neck and torso. Flexibility surprising despite vast toughness.

At bottom of torso rough but dissimilarly functioning counterparts of head arrangements exist. Bulbous light-grey pseudo-neck, without gill suggestions holds greenish five-pointed starfish-arrangement. Tough muscular arms 4 feet long and tapering from 7 inches diameter at base to about 2.5 at point. To each point is attached small end of a greenish five-veined membraneous triangle 8 inches long and 6 wide at farther end. This is the paddle, fin, or pseudo-foot which has made prints in rocks from a thousand million to fifty or sixty million years old…As found, all these projections tightly folded over pseudo-neck and end of torso, corresponding to projections at other end."

The description of the "the Great Old Ones" from which this passage is extracted has remained a classic. If there is a tone one does not expect to find in the horror story, it's that of a dissection report. Other than Lautréamont, who copied the pages of an encyclopedia of animal behavior, it is hard to identify anyone as a predecessor to Lovecraft. And the latter had most certainly never even heard of *Maldoror*. It would seem to be a discovery he made alone: that using science's vocabulary can serve as an extraordinary stimulant to the poetic imagination. The precise, minutely detailed content, dense and theoretical, encyclopedic in its perspective, produces a hallucinatory and thrilling effect.

"At the Mountains of Madness" provides one of the most beautiful examples of such oneiric precision. All place-names are cited, topographic indications abound; each of the settings in the drama is precisely sited by its altitude and longitude. It would be easy to follow the characters' peregrinations on a large-scale map of Antarctica.

The novella's heroes are a team of scientists, which allows for an interesting shift in perspective: Lake's descriptions will encompass animal physiology, those of Pabodie, geology... HPL even allows himself the luxury of including an ardent fan of weird fiction among the team members who regularly quotes passages from *Arthur Gordon Pym*. He is no longer afraid to measure himself up against Poe. In 1923, he was still describing his productions as "gothic horror" and asserting that he was faithful to "invariably the older writers, especially Poe." But he has since moved on. By forcefully introducing the language and concepts of scientific sectors that seem to him to be the weirdest into his tales, he has exploded the casing of the horror story. In any case, that his first published works in France appear in a science-fiction collection seems simply one way of proclaiming him unclassifiable.

It is not just the clinical vocabulary of animal physiology and the more mysterious lexicon of paleontology (Archaean strata that have survived since middle Comanchian times...) that Lovecraft annexed to his universe. He was quick to understand the appeal of linguistic terminology: "The individual, dark-skinned with somewhat reptilian features, expressed himself with hooting emissions and a rapid succession of consonants that brought to mind certain proto-Akkadian dialects."

Archeology and folklore play an equal part in the project from its inception. "We must review all our knowledge, Wilmarth! These frescoes are seven thousand years older than the most ancient Sumerian necropolis!" And HPL never fails to impress as he slips in an allusion to "certain ritual and particularly repugnant customs of the indigenous inhabitants of North Carolina." But what is more astonishing is that he does not limit himself to the human sciences—he tackles the "hard" sciences as well; the most theoretical, those that, *a priori*, are the farthest from a literary universe.

"The Shadow Over Innsmouth" may be the most frightening of Lovecraft's tales; it is built entirely upon the idea of a "frightful and almost unnameable" genetic degeneration. At first affecting the texture of the skin and the manner of pronouncing vowels, its effect is then felt on the general shape of a body, the anatomy, the respiratory and circulatory systems... The predilection for details and the logic of dramatic progression make this truly excruciating reading. Also, notably, genetics is used not merely for its evocative terminology here, but also as the theoretical framework to the story.

Next, HPL plunges swiftly into the then-unexplored resources of mathematics and the physical sciences. He is the first to have understood the poetic impact of topology; to have shuddered in the face of Gödel's work on incomplete systems of formal logic. The vaguely repulsive implications of such strange axiomatic constructs were undoubtedly necessary for the dark entities of the Cthulhu cycle to emerge.

"One man with Oriental eyes has said that all time and space are relative…" This bizarre synthesis of Einstein's work, extracted from "Hypnos" (1922), is but a timid preamble to a theoretical and conceptual unraveling whose apogee is to be found ten years later in "The Dreams in the Witch House," where an attempt will be made to explain the abject circumstances under which an old seventeenth-century woman has "insight into mathematical depths perhaps beyond the utmost modern delvings of Planck, Heisenberg, Einstein, and de Sitter." The angles of the house the unfortunate Walter Gilman inhabits exhibit unsettling peculiarities, inexplicable within the framework of Euclidean geometry. Gilman neglects all the disciplines taught at university other than mathematics, where his genius for resolving Riemannian equations stupefies Professor Upham, who *especially liked his demonstration of the kinship of higher mathematics to certain phases of magical lore transmitted down the ages from an ineffable antiquity—human or pre-human—whose knowledge of the cosmos and its laws was greater than ours."*

Lovecraft, in passing, annexed the equations of quantum mechanics (only barely discovered at the time he was writing) and immediately qualified them as "impious and paradoxical." Walter Gilman dies, his heart devoured by a rat hailing from regions of the cosmos "outside the given space-time continuum."

In his final stories, Lovecraft uses the multiform descriptive methods of science: the obscure memory of fertility rites practiced by a degenerate Tibetan tribe, the baffling algebraic particularities of pre-Hilbertian spaces, an analysis of the genetic derivations of a population of semi-amorphous Chilean lizards, the obscene incantation of a work on demonology compiled by a half-mad Franciscan monk, the unpredictable behavior of a group of neutrinos undergoing exposure to an ever-expanding magnetic field, the hideous and never-before-exhibited sculptures of an English decadent… These all serve to evoke a multifaceted universe where the most heterogeneous fields of knowledge intersect and converge to generate the poetic trance that accompanies the revelation of forbidden truths.

The sciences, in their massive effort to describe the real *objectively,* furnished him with the tools he needed to transmit his vision. Indeed, HPL's aim was objective terror. A terror unbound from any human or psychological connotations. He wished, as he said himself, to create a mythology that "would mean something to those intelligent beings that consist only of nebulous spiraling gases."

Just as Kant hoped to set the foundation of a valid ethical code "not just for man but for all rational beings," Lovecraft wanted to create a horror capable of terrifying all creatures endowed with reason. Apart from this, the two men had commonalities; both were extremely thin and had a weakness for sweets, both were suspected of perhaps *not being fully human.* Be that as it may, what the "loner of Königsberg" and the "recluse of Providence" have in common is the heroic and paradoxical desire to *go beyond* humanity.

THAT WILL BE LOST
IN THE UNNAMEABLE
ARCHITECTURE OF TIME

The style of scientific reporting adopted by HPL in his later stories operates according to the following principle: *the more monstrous and inconceivable the events and entities described, the more precise and clinical the description.* A scalpel is needed to dissect the unnameable.

Hence all impressionism must be banished to build a vertiginous literature; and without a certain *disproportionality of scale,* without the juxtaposition of the minute and the limitless, the punctual and the infinite, there can be no vertigo.

Which is why, in "At the Mountains of Madness," Lovecraft fairly insists on conveying the latitude and longitude at each point in the drama. While, at the same time, he brings to life entities well beyond the boundaries of our galaxy; at times even beyond our space-time continuum. He wants to create a sense of precarious balance; the characters move between precise coordinates, but they are oscillating at the edge of an abyss.

This has its exact complement in the temporal domain. If distant entities that are several hundred million years old appear in the course of our human history, it is vital to document the exact moments of their appearance. Each is a point of rupture. To allow the unutterable to erupt.

The narrator in "The Shadow Out of Time" is a professor of political economy who comes from an old, "altogether normal" Massachusetts family. Thoughtful, well-balanced, there is nothing predisposing him to the transformation he undergoes on Thursday May 14, 1908. When he gets up, he feels a headache; nonetheless, he goes to his classes as usual. Then the event takes place.

"The collapse occurred about 10.20 A.M., while I was conducting a class in Political Economy VI—history and present tendencies of economics—for juniors and a few sophomores. I began to see strange shapes before my eyes, and to feel that I was in a grotesque room other than the classroom.

My thoughts and speech wandered from my subject, and the students saw that something was gravely amiss. Then I slumped down, unconscious, in my chair, in a stupor from which no one could arouse me. Nor did my rightful faculties again look out upon the daylight of our normal world for five years, four months, and thirteen days."

After a sixteen-and-a-half-hour faint, the professor regains consciousness, but his personality appears to have undergone a subtle change. He exhibits a most stunning ignorance of the most rudimentary daily realities while demonstrating an elaborate knowledge of supernatural events from the farthest past; at times he speaks of the future in terms that elicit the greatest fear. The ironic tone of his remarks at times hints at a secret and complete knowledge of things that lie beneath the surface. Even the play of his facial muscles has completely changed. His family and friends instinctively display a certain repugnance toward him, and his wife finally asks for a divorce, alleging that an alien is "usurping the body of her husband."

Indeed, Professor Peaslee's body has been colonized by the spirit of a member of the Great Race, a race of rugose cone-shaped beings that ruled the planet long before the apparition of man and who are capable of projecting their minds into the future.

The reintegration of the spirit of Nathaniel Wingate Peaslee back into its earthly envelope occurs on September 27, 1913; the transmutation begins at a quarter past eleven and is completed by noon, approximately. The professor's first words after a five-year absence are the exact continuation of the lecture in political economics he was giving his students at the start of the story... a great symmetrical effect, perfect story structure.

The juxtaposition of "three hundred million years ago" and "at a quarter past eleven" is equally typical. The scale factor, the vertigo factor. Again, procedures borrowed from architecture.

Every weird story presents in it the collision of monstrous entities hailing from unimaginable, forbidden worlds with the plane of our ordinary existence. In Lovecraft's work, the trajectory of this collision is traced by a precise and firm line that becomes more dense and more complex as the story progresses, and it is this narrative precision that converts us into believers of the inconceivable.

At times, like in "The Call of Cthulhu," whose structural complexity is surprising and impressive, HPL uses several convergent lines. After a night filled with nightmares, a decadent artist creates a particularly hideous statuette. In this figurine, Professor Angell recognizes a new incarnation of the anthropoid monster that had made such a disturbing impression on the participants of the Archaeological Society in St. Louis seventeen years prior. A police inspector had brought the specimen which he had discovered following an investigation into the persistence of certain voodoo rituals requiring human sacrifice and mutilations. Another participant at the Congress had alluded to the marine idol adored by a certain degenerate Eskimo tribe.

After Professor Angell dies "accidentally," carelessly jostled by a negro sailor in a Providence port, his nephew picks up the threads of the investigation. He collects press clippings and finally, in the *Sydney Bulletin,* he comes across an article that recounts the tale of a shipwrecked New Zealand yacht and the inexplicable death of its crew. The only survivor, Captain Johansen, has gone mad. Professor Angell's nephew travels to Norway to question him; Johansen has died without having regained his sanity, and his widow gives the Professor a manuscript in which he tells of their encounter at sea with an abject and gigantic entity *the exact likeness of the statuette.*

The action unfolds on three continents in the novella, and HPL multiplies the narrative procedures, aiming to give an impression of objectivity: newspaper articles, police reports, accounts of the work of scientific organizations… These all converge toward the final paroxysm: the encounter between the Norwegian captain's unfortunate companions and the grand Cthulhu himself: *"Of the six men who never reached the ship, he thinks two perished of pure fright in that accursed instant. The Thing cannot be described—there is no language for such abysms of shrieking and immemorial lunacy, such eldritch contradictions of all matter, force, and cosmic order."*

Between 4:00 p.m. and 4:15 p.m. a breach occurred in the architecture of time. And through the fissure created, a terrifying entity manifested itself on our earth. *Ph'nglui mglw'nafh Cthulhu R'lyeh wagah'nagl fhtagn!*

The great Cthulhu, master of interior depths, Hastur the destroyer, he who walks on the wind and who must not be named. Nyarlathotep, crawling chaos. The mindless and amorphous Azathoth which blasphemes and bubbles at the center of all infinity. Yog-Sothoth, Azathoth's co-ruler. "All-in-One and One-in-

All." Such are the principle elements of Lovecraft's mythology that were to mark his successors so forcefully and that continue to fascinate today. These are the coordinates of the unnameable.

This is not a coherent mythology, precisely drawn; it is unlike Greco-Roman mythology or this or that magical pantheon whose very clarity and *finitude* is almost reassuring. These Lovecraftian entities remain somewhat tenebrous. He avoids precision with regards to the distribution of their powers and abilities. In fact, their exact nature is beyond the grasp of the human mind. The impious books that pay homage to them and celebrate their cult only do so in confused and contradictory terms. They remain fundamentally *unutterable*. We only get fleeting glimpses of their hideous power; and those humans who seek to know more ineluctably pay in madness or in death.

PART THREE

HOLOCAUST

The twentieth century may come to be recognized as the golden age of epic and fantasy literature, once the morbid mists of feeble avant-gardes dissipate. It has already witnessed the emergence of Howard, Lovecraft, and Tolkien—three radically different universes. Three pillars of *dream literature,* as despised by critics as they are loved by the public.

Who cares? In the end critics always recognize their mistakes; or, to be more exact, in the end critics die and are replaced by others. So, after thirty years of scornful silence, "intellectuals" decided to take an interest in Lovecraft. They concluded that as an individual he was endowed with a truly astonishing imagination (they did after all have to attribute his success to something) but that his style was abominable.

That's a joke. If Lovecraft's style is deplorable, one might as well conclude style is inconsequential in literature; and then move on to some other subject.

All the same, this idiotic point of view can be explained. It must be noted, however, that HPL does not cater to the elegant, subtle, minimalist, and restrained notions of style that, generally speaking, moves these suffragettes. Here is an extract from "Under the Pyramids," for example:

"I saw the horror and unwholesome antiquity of Egypt, and the grisly alliance it has always had with the tombs and temples of the dead. I saw phantom processions of priests with the heads of bulls, falcons, cats and ibises; phantom processions marching interminably through subterraneous labyrinths and avenues of titanic propylaea beside which a man is as a fly, and offering unnameable sacrifices to indescribable gods. Stone colossi marched in endless night and drove herds of grinning androsphinxes down to the shores of illimitable stagnant rivers of pitch. And behind it all I saw the ineffable malignity of primordial necromancy, black and amorphous, and fumbling greedily after me in the darkness."

Such emphatically inflated passages evidently present a stumbling block to erudite readers; but it is imperative to point out that it is these very passages that true fans prefer. Lovecraft has never been rivaled in this register. His way of using mathematical concepts, of precisely indicating the topography of each location of a drama, his mythology, his imaginary demoniac library, have all been borrowed; but no one has ever attempted to imitate these passages where he sets aside all stylistic restraint, where adjectives and adverbs pile upon one another to the point of exasperation, and he utters exclamations of pure delirium such as: *"Hippopotami should not have human hands and crazy torches… men should not have the heads of crocodiles…"* And yet this is the true aim of the work. One might even say that the only reason for the often subtle and elaborate structure of Lovecraft's "great texts" is to lay the groundwork for the stylistic explosion of these passages. Like the hallucinatory confession of Zadok Allen, the alcoholic, half-mad nonagenarian in "The Shadow Over Innsmouth:"

"Hheh, heh, heh, heh! Beginnin' to see, hey? Mebbe ye'd like to a ben me in them days, when I seed things at night aout to sea from the cupalo top o' my haouse. Oh, I kin tell ye, little pitchers hev big ears, an' I wa'n't missin' nothin' o' what was gossiped abaout Cap'n Obed an' the folks aout

to the reef! Heh, heh, heh! Haow abaout the night I took my pa's ship's glass up to the cupalo an' seed the reef a-bristlin' thick with shapes that dove off quick soon's the moon riz? Obed an' the folks was in a dory, but them shapes dove off the far side into the deep water an' never come up... Haow'd ye like to be a little shaver alone up in a cupalo a-watchin' shapes as wa'n't human shapes?... Hey?... Heh, heh, heh, heh..."

What opposes Lovecraft to the representatives of good taste is more than a question of details. HPL would probably have considered a story a failure, if in writing it he did not have a chance to *go overboard* once at least. This can be proven *a contrario* by his pronouncement regarding the work of a peer: "[Henry] James is perhaps too diffuse, too unctuously urbane, and too much addicted to subtleties of speech to realise [sic] fully all the wild and devastating horror in his situations..."

This is all the more striking given that throughout his life Lovecraft was the epitome of the discreet, reserved, well-educated gentleman. Never one to utter a horror, nor to rant in public. No one ever once saw him angry; nor crying; nor laughing out loud. His was a life pared down to the bare minimum whose only animus was literature and dreams. An exemplary life.

ANTIBIOGRAPHY

Howard Phillips Lovecraft serves as example to all who wish to learn how to fail in life and eventually succeed in their work. And even on that score, results are not guaranteed. Practicing a policy of complete non-engagement vis-à-vis vital realities carries with it the risk of plunging into deepest apathy; one might no longer even write—and that is exactly what almost happened to him, several times. Another danger is suicide, which one must learn to negotiate with; thus, over the course of several years, Lovecraft always kept a small bottle of cyanide at hand. This can come to be very useful, so long as one can hold out. He did, but not without difficulty.

First, money. In this regard HPL presents the disconcerting example of an individual who is both poor and disinterested. Without ever quite falling to the depths of utter destitution he was, nevertheless, extremely financially constrained throughout his life. His correspondence painfully reveals how he had to constantly pay attention to the price of each thing, including the most basic consumer items. He was never able to undertake a significant expenditure such as the purchase of a car or the dreamed-about trip to Europe.

The bulk of his income derived from revision and correction work. He accepted work at extremely low rates, virtually for free if it was for friends; and when one of his invoices went unpaid, in general, he abstained from resending it. It was not dignified for a *gentleman* to become involved in sordid money matters or to express too lively an anxiety where his own interests were concerned.

Otherwise, he did dispose of a small sum by inheritance that he nibbled at throughout his life, but it was too meager to amount to more than a small stipend. What's more, it is somewhat poignant to note that at the time of his death this sum had subsided to almost zero; as if he had lived exactly the number of years allotted him by his (rather feeble) family fortune and his own (rather strong) ability to economize.

As for his own works, they brought him almost nothing. In any case, he did not consider it proper to make a profession of literature. As he writes, "a gentleman shouldn't write all his images down for a plebian rabble to stare at." The sincerity of such a declaration is obviously difficult to appreciate; it might appear to us to be the consequence of a formidable web of inhibitions, but one must also consider it to be a rigid interpretation of the obsolete code of conduct to which Lovecraft adhered with all his might. He always wished to see himself as a country gentleman, cultivating literature as one of the fine arts, for the sake of his own pleasure and that of a few friends, without worrying about the public's taste, fashionable themes, or anything else of the kind. Such a character no longer has a place in our society; he knew this, but always refused to take it into account. And, anyhow, what set him apart from a true "country gentleman" is that he owned nothing, but this, too, he did not wish to acknowledge.

In an age of frenzied commercialism it is a comfort to see one who so obstinately refused to "sell himself." Here, for example, is the letter he attached to the first manuscript he sent to *Weird Tales* in 1923:

> *"Dear sir,*
>
> *Having a habit of writing weird, macabre and fantastic stories for my own amusement, I have largely been simultaneously hounded by nearly a dozen well-meaning friends into deciding to submit a few of these Gothic horrors to your newly founded periodical. Enclosed are five tales written between 1917 and 1923.*
>
> *Of these the first two are probably the best. If they be unsatisfactory, the rest need not be read...*
>
> *[...]*
>
> *I have no idea that these things will be found suitable for I pay no attention to the demands of commercial writing. My object is such pleasure as I can obtain from the creation of certain bizarre pictures, situations, or atmospheric effects; and the only reader I hold in mind is myself.*
>
> *My models are invariably the older writers, especially Poe, who has been my favourite literary figure since early childhood. Should any miracle impel you to consider the publication of my tales, I have but one condition to offer and that is that no excisions be made. If the tale cannot be printed as written, down to the very last semicolon and comma, it must gracefully accept rejection. Excision by others is probably one reason why no living American author has a real prose style... but I am probably safe for my MSS are not likely to win your consideration. 'Dagon' has been rejected by* Black Mask *to which I sent it under external compulsion—much as I am sending you the enclosed."*

Lovecraft was to change with regard to many points, especially his devotion to the style of the "old writers." But he remained steadfastly proud and masochistic, and his fiercely anticommercial streak never varied: he refused to type his texts, he sent editors dirty, crumpled manuscripts, and he systematically disclosed all his prior rejections... He did everything to displease. No concessions. Here too, he played against himself.

"Of course, I am unfamiliar with amatory phenomenon save through cursory reading."

Letter to Rheinhart Kleiner, September 27, 1919

Lovecraft's biography presents very few events. *"Nothing ever happens"* is the leitmotif of his letters. But it can be stated that this life, already so pared down, would have been rigorously empty had he not crossed paths with Sonia Haft Greene.

Like him, she belonged to the "amateur journalism" movement. Around 1920 this movement was very active in the United States, and brought a number of isolated writers, who were outside the usual network of publishing, the satisfaction of seeing their work in print, distributed, and read. This was Lovecraft's only social activity; it brought him all his friends, and also his wife.

When she met him, she was thirty-eight years old, in other words seven years his senior. She was divorced, had a sixteen-year-old daughter from her first marriage, lived in New York, and earned her living as a saleswoman in a clothing store.

She appears to have immediately fallen in love with him. For his part, Lovecraft maintained a somewhat aloof attitude. In reality, he knew nothing about women. She had to take the first step as well as the ones that followed. She invited him to dinner, came to visit him in Providence. Finally, in a small Rhode Island village called Magnolia, she took the initiative and kissed him. Lovecraft blushed, turned pale. When Sonia gently teased him, he had to explain to her that it was the first time since his tender childhood years that he had been kissed.

This was in 1922, when Lovecraft was thirty-two years old. He and Sonia were married two years later. With the passing months he seems to have progressively decongealed. Sonia Greene was an exceptionally sweet and charming woman—general opinion indicates she was also a very attractive woman. And the unthinkable took place, the "old gentleman" fell in love.

Later, after the failure of their marriage, Sonia destroyed all the letters Lovecraft had written her. Only one remains, bizarrely pathetic in its wish to fathom human love, written by one who feels himself to be so very far from humanity in every way. Here are a few brief passages from it:

> "Dear Mrs. Greene:
> The mutual love of man and woman for one another is an imaginative experience that consists of having its object bear a certain special relation to the aesthetic-emotional life of its possessor...
>
> "With long years of slowly nurtured love comes adaptation and perfect adjustment; memories, dream-pictures, delicate, aesthetic stimuli and usual impressions of dream-beauty become permanent modifications through the influence of which each tacitly exercises upon the other.
>
> "There is a universal difference between the romances of youth and of maturity. By forty or perhaps fifty a wholesome replacement process begins

to operate, and love attains calm, cool depths based on tender association beside which the erotic infatuation of youth takes on a certain shade of cheapness and degradation."

Theoretically speaking, these considerations are not incorrect; they simply appear somewhat misplaced. Let's just say that as a whole it is a somewhat unusual love letter. All the same, this blatant anti-eroticism does not hinder Sonia. She feels capable of coming to terms with her bizarre lover's reticence. There is, in relationships between human beings, an element of pure mystery, particularly remarkable in this case. Sonia appears to have understood Lovecraft perfectly, his frigidity, his inhibitions, his refusal of and aversion to life. As for him, who at thirty considered himself an old man, it's amazing that he was able to envision a partnership with such a dynamic, lush, lively being. A divorced Jew, no less—which for a conservative anti-Semite such as him must have presented something of an insurmountable obstacle.

It has been suggested that he might have wished to be supported financially. Although this is not necessarily a far-fetched idea, the turn events were to take must have cruelly belied such a project. Of course, as a writer, he may have given in to the temptation to "acquire new experiences" regarding sexuality and marriage. Finally, one must remember that it was Sonia who made all the first moves and that Lovecraft was never capable of saying no with regard to any matter whatsoever. But, there is yet another and more unlikely explanation that might appear to be the best: Lovecraft seems to have been in love with Sonia *in a certain way*, just as Sonia was in love with him. And these two dissimilar beings, who nonetheless loved one another, were united by the ties of matrimony on March 3, 1924.

THE SHOCK OF NEW YORK

Immediately after their marriage, the couple began living in Brooklyn in Sonia's apartment. Lovecraft was to spend two of the most surprising years of his life there. The misanthropic and slightly sinister recluse from Providence was transformed into an affable, lively man, ever ready for an outing to a restaurant or a museum. He sent enthusiastic letters announcing his marriage:

"Two are joined to form but one. Another will now bear the Lovecraft name. A new family is founded!"

"I wish you could behold Grandpa this week, getting up regularly in the daytime, hustling briskly about,... And all this with a prospect of regular literary work—my first real job—in the offing."

His correspondents came to visit him; the Lovecrafts' apartment was never empty. They were all taken aback when they met a young man of thirty-four where they had expected to find a disenchanted old man. Lovecraft at this point was equally surprised. He even began to entertain dreams of literary celebrity and to contact editors, to entertain the possibility of *success*. This miracle bore Sonia's signature.

He didn't even miss the colonial architecture of Providence

that he had considered so indispensable to his survival. On the contrary, his first contact with New York was marked by a sense of awe, echoes of which can be found in "He," a largely autobiographical story written in 1925:

"Coming for the first time upon the town, I had seen it in the sunset from a bridge, majestic above its waters, its incredible peaks and pyramids rising flower-like and delicate from pools of violet mist to play with the flaming golden clouds and the first stars of evening. Then it had lighted up window by window above the shimmering tides where lanterns nodded and glided and deep horns bayed weird harmonies, and itself become a starry firmament of dream redolent of faery music…"

Lovecraft had never been so close to happiness as in that year of 1924. Had their union lasted… Had he been able to find a job as the editor of *Weird Tales*… He might have…

But, it would all fall apart after a minor event with considerable consequences: Sonia lost her job. She tried opening her own boutique, but the business went under. As a result, Lovecraft was forced to look for work in order to ensure the subsistence of their household.

This proved to be an absolutely impossible task. Nonetheless, he tried—he answered hundreds of job offers, applied for other jobs spontaneously… it was all a complete failure. Of course. He had no understanding of the realities behind words such as dynamic, competitive, commercial sense, efficiency… Still, in an economy that at the time was not even in crisis, he should have been able to find at least a subordinate position somewhere… But, no. Nothing at all. Apparently in the American economy of his era, there was absolutely no conceivable place for an individual like Lovecraft. This is a kind of *mystery;* and he himself, while quite aware of his eccentricity and his deficiencies, did not quite understand it.

Here is an extract of the circular letter he ended up writing to "potential employers":

"The notion that not even a man of cultivation & good intelligence

can possibly acquire rapid effectiveness in a field ever so slightly outside his own routine, would seem to be a naïve one; yet recent events have shown me most emphatically what a widespread superstition it is. Since commencing two months ago, a quest for work for which I am naturally & scholastically well fitted, I have answered nearly a hundred advertisements without gaining so much as one chance for satisfactory hearing—& all, apparently because I cannot point to previous employment in the precise industrial subdivision represented by the various firms. Faring thus with the usual channels, I am at last experimentally taking the aggressive."

The vaguely burlesque nature of the endeavor *("experimentally,"* for instance) should not mask the fact that Lovecraft found himself to be in a truly dire financial situation. And that his repeated failures were a surprise to him. Although he may have been vaguely aware that he was not altogether in step with the society of his day, he nonetheless had not expected such utter rejection. Further along, the distress pierces through when he announces that he is *"willing, in deference to custom & necessity, to begin most modestly, & with the small remuneration which novices usually receive."* But there was nothing at all. No matter what the remuneration, his applications were of interest to no one. He was inadaptable to the market economy. And he began to sell his furniture.

At the same time, his attitude toward his environment deteriorated. You have to be poor to truly understand New York. And Lovecraft was about to discover what lay behind the curtain. These paragraphs follow the earlier description of the city in "He":

"But success and happiness were not to be. Garish daylight shewed only squalor and alienage and the noxious elephantiasis of climbing, spreading stone where the moon had hinted of loveliness and elder magic; and the throngs of people that seethed through the flume-like streets were squat, swarthy strangers with hardened faces and narrow eye, shrewd strangers without dreams and without kinship to the scenes about them, who could never mean aught to a blue-eyed man of the old folk with the love of fair green lanes and white New England village steeples in his heart."

Here are the first hints of the racism that later nourishes HPL's body of work. It first appears in a most banal form: unemployed, threatened by poverty, Lovecraft had more and more trouble tolerating the hard and aggressive urban environment. Furthermore, he began to feel bitterness toward immigrants of diverse origins, who he saw blending easily into the swirling *melting pot* that was America in the 1920s, while he himself, in spite of his pure Anglo-Saxon origins, was unable to find any work. But there was more. There was more to come.

On December 31, 1924, Sonia left for Cincinnati, where she found a new job. Lovecraft refused to accompany her. He could not bear to be exiled in an anonymous Midwestern city. At any rate, he no longer believed in it—and he began to consider a return to Providence. One can follow the evolution of this process in "He": *"With this mode of relief I even wrote a few poems, and still refrained from going home to my people lest I seem to crawl back ignobly in defeat."*

He nonetheless remained in New York a little over a year. Sonia lost her job in Cincinnati but found another in Cleveland. American mobility… She returned home every two weeks and brought her husband the money necessary to survive. And he continued in vain his pitiful search for employment. In fact he felt awful about it all. He would have liked to return home to Providence to his aunts, but he did not dare. For the very first time in his life it was impossible for him to behave as a *gentleman*. Here is how he described Sonia's attitude to his aunt Lillian Clark:

"I have never beheld a more admirable attitude of disinterested & solicitous regard; in which each financial shortcoming is accepted & condoned as soon as it is proved inevitable, & in which acquiescence is extended even to my statements (as determined by my observation of the effect of varying conditions on my nerves) that the one essential ingredient

of my life is a certain amount of quiet & freedom for creative literary composition… A devotion which can accept this combination of incompetence & aesthetic selfishness without a murmur contrary tho' it must be to all expectations originally entertained; is assuredly a phenomenon so rare & so akin to the historic quality of saintliness, that no one with the least sense of artistic proportion could possibly meet it with other than the keenest reciprocal esteem, respect, admiration, & affection…"

Poor Lovecraft, poor Sonia. The inevitable happened all the same, and in April 1926 Lovecraft abandoned the New York apartment and returned to Providence to live at his older aunt Lillian Clark's house. He was to divorce Sonia three years later—and would never know another woman. In 1926, his life had for all intents and purposes ended. His veritable body of work—the "grand texts" series—was about to get underway.

New York had marked him forever. During the course of 1925, his hatred of the "foul mongrels" of this modern Babylon, the "foreign colossus that gibbers and howls vulgarly…" did not cease to exasperate him and drove him delirious. It could even be posited that a fundamental figure in his body of work—the idea of a grand, titanic city, in whose foundations crawl repugnant nightmare beings—sprang directly from his New York experience.

RACIAL HATRED

Lovecraft had in fact always been a racist. But in his youth this racism did not go beyond what was acceptable within his social class—that of the puritanical Protestant old bourgeoisie of New England. Along these same lines, he was also by nature *reactionary* in every regard, be it verse technique or young girl's dresses, he valued orderly, traditional notions over freer, progressive ones. There is nothing especially outstanding or eccentric about this. He was just particularly *old-fashioned*. It seemed self-evident to him that Anglo-Saxon Protestants were by nature entitled to the highest positions within the social order; as to other races (he really barely knew any other races, and had no wish to become acquainted with them), he only felt a distant and benevolent disdain toward them. Let each stick to his own station in life, avoid all thoughtless novelty and all will be well.

Disdain is not a productive literary sentiment; generally, it results only in well-bred silence. But Lovecraft was forced to live in New York, where he came to know hatred, disgust, and fear, otherwise stimulating sentiments. And it was in New York that his racist opinions turned into a full-fledged racist neurosis. Being poor, he was forced to live in the same neighborhoods as the "obscene, repulsive, nightmarish" immigrants. He would brush past them on streets and in public parks. He was jostled by "greasy sneering half-castes," by "hideous negroes that resemble gigantic chimpanzees" in the subway. And in the long lines of job seekers he came across them again and realized to his horror that his own aristocratic bearing and refined education tempered with his "balanced conservatism" brought him no advantage. His currency was worth nothing here in Babylon; here wiles and brute force reigned supreme, here "rat-faced Jews" and "monstrous half-breeds skip about rolling on their heels absurdly."

This is no longer the WASP's well-bred racism; it is the brutal hatred of a trapped animal who is forced to share his cage with other different and frightening creatures. Still, his hypocrisy and good manners last till the end, as he writes to his aunt that individuals of their background must not stand out by their speech or by any inconsiderate actions. According to those close to him, when he crossed paths with members of other races Lovecraft grated his teeth and turned rather pale, but would keep calm. It was only in his letters that his exasperation poured forth—later it showed up in his stories and eventually became something of a phobia. His sight, nourished as it was by hatred, grew into paranoia and eventually his gaze was actually deranged, portending the verbal hyperbole of the "great texts." Here, for example, is how he describes the Lower East Side and its immigrant population to Belknap Long:

"The organic things—Italo-Semitico-Mongoloid—inhabiting that awful cesspool could not by any stretch of the imagination be call'd human. They were monstrous and nebulous adumbrations of the pithecanthropoid and amoebal; vaguely moulded from some stinking viscous slime of earth's corruption, and slithering and oozing in and on the filthy streets or in and out of windows and doorways in a fashion suggestive of nothing but infesting worms or deep-sea unnamabilities. They—or the degenerate gelatinous fermentation of which they were composed—seem'd to ooze, seep and

trickle thro' the gaping cracks in the horrible houses… and I thought of some avenue of Cyclopean and unwholesome vats, crammed to the vomiting-point with gangrenous vileness, and about to burst and inundate the world in one leprous cataclysm of semi-fluid rottenness.

From that nightmare of perverse infection I could carry away the memory of any living face. The individually grotesque was lost in the collectively devastating; which left on the eye only the broad, phantasmal linements of the morbid mould of disintegration and decay… a yellow and leering mask with sour, sticky, acid ichors oozing at eyes, ears, nose, and mouth, and abnormally bubbling from monstrous and unbelievable sores at every point…"

Indisputably great Lovecraftian prose. But what race could possibly have provoked this outburst? He himself no longer knew; at one point he mentions the "Italico-Semitico-Mongoloids." The ethnic realities at play had long been wiped out; what is certain is that he hated them all and was incapable of any greater specificity.

His descriptions of the nightmare entities that populate the Cthulhu cycle spring directly from this hallucinatory vision. Racial hatred provokes in Lovecraft the trancelike poetic state in which he outdoes himself by the mad rhythmic pulse of cursed sentences; this is the source of the hideous and cataclysmic light that illuminates his final works. The association is clear in "The Horror at Red Hook."

The longer Lovecraft was forced to remain in New York against his will, the greater his repulsion and his terror, until they reached alarming proportions. Thus he would write to Belknap Long, "the New York mongoloid problem is beyond calm mention." Further on in the letter he declares, "I hope the end *will* be warfare…" In another letter, in a sinister presage he advocates the use of cyanide gas.

His return to Providence hardly helped matters. Prior to going to New York, he had not even suspected that foreign creatures could be slithering onto the streets of this charming provincial city; he most likely had passed by them without ever seeing them. But now his gaze was endowed with a painful acuity; and even in those beloved neighborhoods he found the first stigmata of this "leprosy": *"Oozing out of various apertures and dragging themselves along the narrow lanes are shapeless forms of organic entity…"*

However, gradually, this sanctuary to which he was able to retreat away from society produced its effect. By avoiding all visual contact with the foreign races he regained his equanimity to some extent. His admiration for Hitler subsided. Where once he'd seen him as an elemental force called to regenerate European culture, he came to see him as "a clown," and then, to concede that although his objectives were fundamentally sane, the absurd extremism of his then-current policy risked leading to disastrous results that directly contradicted his original principles.

Concurrently, the calls to massacre became more infrequent. He had written in a letter "either stow 'em out of sight or kill 'em off," and he gradually came to consider the first solution to be preferable, especially after a stay in the South at the home of the writer Robert Barlow, where he was shocked to assess that rigorous racial segregation allowed a white, educated American to feel at ease amongst a majority black population. "Of course," he clarified, in a letter to his aunt, "they can't let niggers use the beach at a Southern resort—can you imagine sensitive persons bathing near a pack of chimpanzees?"

The role of this racial hatred in Lovecraft's body of work has often been underestimated. Only Francis Lacassin has had the courage to put the question honestly; in his preface to the *Letters* he writes: "The myths of Cthulhu draw their cold power from the sadistic delectation with which Lovecraft subjects humans, punished for their resemblance to the New York rabble that had humiliated him, to the persecution of beings come from the stars." This remark seems extremely profound to me, even though it is incorrect. What is indisputable is that Lovecraft, as it is sometimes said of boxers, was "full of rage." But it must be stated unequivocally that in his stories the role of the victim is generally played by an Anglo-Saxon university professor who is refined, reserved, and well-educated. Someone who, in fact, is rather like himself. As for the torturers, servants of innumerable cults, they are almost always half-breeds, mulattos, of mixed blood, among the basest of species. In Lovecraft's universe cruelty is not an intellectual refinement, it is a bestial impulse that perfectly reflects the darkest stupidity. As for the courteous, refined individuals characterized by their great delicacy of manner... they provide the perfect victims.

So the central passion animating his work is much more akin to masochism than to sadism; which only underscores its dangerous profundity. As Antonin Artaud noted, cruelty toward another can only produce a mediocre outcome; cruelty conferred upon oneself, on the other hand, is of an altogether different order of interest.

It is true, HPL occasionally manifests an admiration for the "blond beast of eternal snows and frozen oceans." But it is most certainly a bitter sort of admiration; he feels extremely distant from these beings and, unlike Howard, never envisioned putting them in his work. In response to the young Belknap Long, who gently teased him for his admiration for the "great blond beasts of prey," he wrote with marvelous frankness: "You are perfectly right in saying that it is the weak who tend to worship the strong. That is my case exactly." He knew perfectly well that there was no part for him in any heroic Valhalla of battles and conquests other than that of the vanquished, as usual. He was pierced to the core by his failures, by what seemed like his wholly natural and fundamental predisposition to failure. And in his literary universe, too, there could be only one part for him: that of the victim.

HOW WE CAN LEARN FROM HOWARD PHILLIPS LOVECRAFT TO TURN OUR SPIRIT INTO A LIVING SACRIFICE

Lovecraft's heroes strip themselves of life. Renouncing all human joy, they become pure intellects, pure spirits striving toward a single goal: the search for knowledge. At the end of their quest, a terrifying revelation awaits them: from the swamps of Louisiana to the frozen plateaus of the Antarctic desert, in the very heart of New York and in the somber vales of Vermont's countryside, everything proclaims *the universal presence of evil*.

"*Nor is it to be thought that man is either the oldest or the last of earth's masters, or that the common bulk of life and substance walks alone. The Old Ones were, the Old Ones are, and the Old Ones shall be. Not in the spaces we know, but between them, they walk serene and primal, undimensioned and to us unseen.*"

Evil, in all its aspects; instinctively adored by cunning degenerate populations who have composed terrifying hymns to its glory.

"*Yog-Sothoth is the gate. Yog-Sothoth is the key and guardian of the gate. Past, present, future, all are one in Yog-Sothoth. He knows where the Old Ones broke through of old and where They shall break through again. [...] The wind gibbers with Their voices and the earth mutters with Their consciousness. They bend the forest and crush the city, yet may not forest or city behold the hand that smites. Kadath in the cold waste hath known Them, and what man knows Kadath? [...] As a foulness shall ye know Them. Their hand is at your throats, yet ye see Them not; and Their habitation is even one with your guarded threshold. Yog-Sothoth is the key to the gate, whereby the spheres meet. Man rules now where They ruled once; They shall soon rule where Man rules now. After summer is winter, and after winter summer. They wait patient and potent, for here shall They reign again."*

This magnificent invocation calls for several remarks. First, Lovecraft was a poet; he is amongst those writers who *began with poetry*. The first quality apparent in his work was the harmonious rhythm of his sentences; the rest was to come later, and after much work.

Next, it has to be said that these stanzas to all-powerful Evil sound disagreeably familiar. In general, Lovecraft's mythology is very original, but at times it appears to be a frightful inversion of Christian themes. This is particularly the case in "The Dunwich Horror," in which an illiterate peasant woman who has known no men gives birth to a monstrous creature endowed with superhuman powers. This inverted incarnation ends with a repugnant parody of the Passion where the creature, sacrificed at the summit of a mountain that overlooks Dunwich, cries out desperately, *"Father! Father! YOG-SOTHOTH!"* in a faithful echo of *"Eloi, Eloi, Lama Sabachthani."* Here, Lovecraft goes back to a very ancient source of horror where Evil is the product of a carnal union against nature. This idea fits his obsessive racism perfectly; for, to him, as to all racists, it is not one particular race that represents true horror, but the notion of the half-breed. Using both his knowledge of genetics and his familiarity with sacred texts, he concocts an explosive synthesis of abject, unprecedented force. To Christ, the new Adam come to regenerate mankind, Lovecraft opposes the "negro" who has come to regenerate humanity through bestiality and vice. "The time would be easy to know, for then mankind would have become as the Great Old Ones…" This is just a frightening paraphrasing of Saint Paul.

Here we approach what lies beneath Lovecraft's racism; he who designated himself the victim and who picked his tor-mentors. He felt no doubts regarding this topic: "sensitive persons" would be vanquished by "greasy chimpanzees," they would be pul-verized, tortured, and devoured, their bodies would be torn apart in ignoble rites to the obsessive rhythm of ecstatic drumbeats. Already the varnish of civilization was cracking; the forces of Evil await "patient and potent" because they are going to regenerate again on earth.

Underlying these ruminations on the decay of cultures, which are merely a superimposed layer of intellectual justification, is fear. Fear from afar, preceded by repulsion—it is what generates indig-nation and hatred.

Dressed in their rigid, rather grim clothes, accustomed to repressing their emotions and desires, the Protestant Puritans of New England may have at times succeeded in forgetting their ani-mal origin. Which is why Lovecraft consents to their company, but even then, only in moderate doses. Their very insignificance is reassuring. But in the presence of "negroes" he experiences an irrepressible reaction of his nervous system. Their vitality, their apparent lack of complexes or inhibitions, terrifies and repulses him. They dance in the street, they listen to music, rhythmic music… They talk out loud. They laugh in public. Life seems to amuse them, which is worrying. Because life is itself evil.

AGAINST THE WORLD,
AGAINST LIFE

More so today than ever before, Lovecraft would have been a misfit and a recluse. Born in 1890, he already appeared to his contemporaries, in the years of his youth, to be an obsolete reactionary. It's not hard to imagine what he would have thought of our society today. Since his death, it has not ceased evolving in a direction which could only have led him to hate it more. Mechanization and modernization have ineluctably destroyed the lifestyle he was attached to with his every fiber (it is not as if he harbored any delusions about humanity's ability to influence events; as he wrote in a letter, "Everything in modern existence is a direct & absolute corollary of the discoveries of applied steam power & of large-scale applications of electrical energy.") The ideals of liberty and of democracy that he so abhorred have spread all over the planet. The man who declared: "What we detest is sim-ply *change* itself" could only have bristled at the degree to which the idea of progress has come to be an indisputable and almost unconscious credo. The reach of liberal capitalism has extended over minds; in step and hand in hand with it are mercantilism, publicity, the absurd and sneering cult of economic efficiency, the exclusive and immoderate appetite for material riches. Worse still, liberalism has spread from the domain of economics to the domain of sexuality. Every sentimental fiction has been eradicated. Purity, chastity, fidelity, and decency are ridiculous stigmas. The value of a human being today is measured in terms of his economic efficiency and his erotic potential—that is to say, in terms of the two things that Lovecraft most despised.

Horror writers are reactionaries in general simply because they are particularly, one might even say *professionally,* aware of the existence of Evil. It is somewhat curious that among Lovecraft's numerous disciples none has been struck by this simple fact: the evolution of the modern world has made Lovecraftian phobias ever more present, ever more *alive.*

Robert Bloch, one of his youngest correspondents (when they exchanged their first letters he was fifteen), is an exception. His best stories are ones where he pours forth his hatred of the modern world, of youth, of liberated women, of rock, etc. Jazz already appears to him to be a decadent obscenity; as for rock, Bloch interprets it as a return to the most apish savagery endorsed by the hypocritical amorality of progressive intellectuals. In "Sweet Sixteen," a band of Hells Angels, simply described at the outset as ultraviolent hoodlums, carry out sacrificial rites on the daughter of an anthropologist. Rock, beer, and cruelty. This works perfectly, is perfectly coherent, perfectly justified. But such attempts at inserting the demoniac into a modern setting remain exceptional. And Robert Bloch's realist writing and the attention he brings to his characters' social background is clearly set apart from the influence of HPL. Of those writers with a more direct link to the Lovecraftian movement, none adopted and appropriated the master's reactionary racial phobias.

True, this is a treacherous path that only leads to narrow straits. Not because of censorship or litigation. Horror writers probably feel that marked hostility toward any form of freedom in the end breeds hostility to life itself. Lovecraft felt the same way, but he did not stop halfway; he was an extremist. That the world was evil, intrinsically evil, evil by its very essence, was a conclusion he had no trouble reaching, and this was also the most profound meaning of his admiration for Puritans. What amazed him about them was that they "hated life and scorned the platitude that it is worth living." We shall traverse this vale of tears that separates birth from death; but we must remain pure. HPL in no way shared the hopes of Puritans; but he shared their refusal. He explained his point of view in a letter to Belknap Long (written, moreover, only a few days before his marriage):

"And as for Puritan inhibitions—I admire them more every day. They are attempts to make of life a work of art—to fashion a pattern of beauty in the hog-wallow that is animal existence—and they spring out of that divine hatred of life which marks the deepest and most sensitive soul."

Toward the end of his days he did come to at times express poignant regrets in the face of the solitude and failure of his existence. But his regrets remained, if one might express them thus, *theoretical*. He remembered the periods in his life (the end of adolescence, the brief and decisive interval of marriage) where his path might clearly have bifurcated toward what is called happiness. But he understood that he was probably incapable of behaving any other way. And in the end, like Schopenhauer, he concluded that he hadn't fared too badly.

He faced death with courage. Struck by intestinal cancer that spread to his entire upper body, he was transported on March 10, 1937, to the Jane Brown Memorial Hospital. He was an exemplary patient, polite, affable, whose stoicism and courtesy impressed all the nurses, in spite of his very intense physical suffering (thankfully attenuated by morphine). He underwent the pangs of death with resignation and perhaps with a certain secret satisfaction. This life that was leaving behind its carnal envelope was his old enemy; he had denigrated it, fought it, he would not utter a single word of regret. And he passed away, without further incident, on March 15, 1937.

As biographers have said, "Lovecraft died, his work was born." And indeed, we have just begun to put him in his true place, equal or superior to that of Edgar Poe—in any event, resolutely unique. In the face of the repeated failure of his literary creations, he at times felt the sacrifice of his life had actually been in vain. Today we can pronounce a different judgment; we can, for he has been our essential guide, taking us on initiatory journeys to *different* universes that lie somewhere well beyond the limits of human experience, but that provoke in us a precise and terrible emotional impact.

This man, who did not succeed at life, did indeed succeed at writing. It was hard for him. It took him years. New York helped him. He who was so gentle, so courteous, discovered hatred there. Returning to Providence he composed the magnificent tales that vibrate like incantations, that are as precise as a dissection. The dramatic structure of the "great texts" is impressively complex; the narrative procedures are precise, new and bold. Perhaps all this would not suffice were it not that at the center of the ensemble, one feels the power of a consuming interior force.

Every great passion, be it love or hate, will in the end generate an authentic work. One may deplore it, but one must recognize it: Lovecraft was more on the side of hate; of hate and fear. The universe, which intellectually he perceived as being indifferent, became hostile aesthetically. His own existence, which might have been nothing but the sum of banal disappointments, turned into a surgical operation, and an inverted celebration.

The work of his mature years remains faithful to the physical prostration of his youth, transfiguring it. This is the profound secret of Lovecraft's genius, and the pure source of his poetry: he succeeded in transforming his aversion for life into an *effective* hostility.

To offer an alternative to life in all its forms constitutes a permanent opposition, a permanent recourse to life—this is the poet's highest mission on this earth. Howard Phillips Lovecraft fulfilled this mission.

THE CALL
OF CTHULHU
(1926)

by H. P. LOVECRAFT

(Found Among the Papers of the Late
Francis Wayland Thurston, of Boston)

"*Of such great powers or beings there may be conceivably a survival… a survival of a hugely remote period when… consciousness was manifested, perhaps, in shapes and forms long since withdrawn before the tide of advancing humanity… forms of which poetry and legend alone have caught a flying memory and called them gods, monsters, mythical beings of all sorts and kinds….*"   —Algernon Blackwood.

I. THE HORROR IN CLAY.

The most merciful thing in the world, I think, is the inability of the human mind to correlate all its contents. We live on a placid island of ignorance in the midst of black seas of infinity, and it was not meant that we should voyage far. The sciences, each straining in its own direction, have hitherto harmed us little; but some day the piecing together of dissociated knowledge will open up such terrifying vistas of reality, and of our frightful position therein, that we shall either go mad from the revelation or flee from the deadly light into the peace and safety of a new dark age.

Theosophists have guessed at the awesome grandeur of the cosmic cycle wherein our world and human race form transient incidents. They have hinted at strange survivals in terms which would freeze the blood if not masked by a bland optimism. But it is not from them that there came the single glimpse of forbidden aeons which chills me when I think of it and maddens me when I dream of it. That glimpse, like all dread glimpses of truth, flashed out from an accidental piecing together of separated things—in this case an old newspaper item and the notes of a dead professor. I hope that no one else will accomplish this piecing out; certainly, if I live, I shall never knowingly supply a link in so hideous a chain. I think that the professor, too intented to keep silent regarding the part he knew, and that he would have destroyed his notes had not sudden death seized him.

My knowledge of the thing began in the winter of 1926-27 with the death of my grand-uncle, George Gammell Angell, Professor Emeritus of Semitic Languages in Brown University, Providence, Rhode Island. Professor Angell was widely known as an authority on ancient inscriptions, and had frequently been resorted to by the heads of prominent museums; so that his passing at the age of ninety-two may be recalled by many. Locally, interest was intensified by the obscurity of the cause of death. The professor had been stricken whilst returning from the Newport boat; falling suddenly; as witnesses said, after having been jostled by a nautical-looking negro who had come from one of the queer dark courts on the precipitous hillside which formed a short cut from the waterfront to the deceased's home in Williams Street. Physicians were unable to find any visible disorder, but concluded after perplexed debate that some obscure lesion of the heart, induced by the brisk ascent of so steep a hill by so elderly a man, was responsible for the end. At the time I saw no reason to dissent from this dictum, but latterly I am inclined to wonder—and more than wonder.

As my grand-uncle's heir and executor, for he died a childless widower, I was expected to go over his papers with some thoroughness; and for that purpose moved his entire set of files and boxes to my quarters in Boston. Much of the material which I correlated will be later published by the American Archaeological Society, but there was one box which I found exceedingly puzzling, and which I felt much averse from shewing to other eyes. It had been locked and I did not find the key till it occurred to me to examine the personal ring which the professor carried in his pocket. Then, indeed, I succeeded in opening it, but when I did so seemed only to be confronted by a greater and more closely locked barrier. For what could be the meaning of the queer clay bas-relief and the disjointed jottings, ramblings, and cuttings which I found? Had my uncle, in his latter years, become credulous of the most superficial impostures? I resolved to search out the eccentric sculptor responsible for this apparent disturbance of an old man's peace of mind.

The bas-relief was a rough rectangle less than an inch thick and about five by six inches in area; obviously of modern origin. Its designs, however, were far from modern in atmosphere and suggestion; for, although the vagaries of cubism and futurism are many and wild, they do not often reproduce that cryptic regularity which lurks in prehistoric writing. And writing of some kind the bulk of these designs seemed certainly to be; though my memory, despite much familiarity with the papers and collections of my uncle, failed in any way to identify this particular species, or even hint at its remotest affiliations.

Above these apparent hieroglyphics was a figure of evident pictorial intent, though its impressionistic execution forbade a very clear idea of its nature. It seemed to be a sort of monster, or symbol representing a monster, of a form which only a diseased fancy could conceive. If I say that my somewhat extravagant imagination yielded simultaneous pictures of an octopus, a dragon, and a human caricature, I shall not be unfaithful to the spirit of the thing. A pulpy, tentacled head surmounted a grotesque and scaly body with rudimentary wings; but it was the *general outline* of the whole which made it most shockingly frightful. Behind the figure was a vague suggestions of a Cyclopean architectural background.

The writing accompanying this oddity was, aside from a stack of press cuttings, in Professor Angell's most recent hand; and made no pretense to literary style. What seemed to be the main document was headed "CTHULHU CULT" in characters painstakingly printed to avoid the erroneous reading of a word so unheard-of. The manuscript was divided into two sections, the first of which was headed "1925—Dream and Dream Work of H.A. Wilcox, 7 Thomas St., Providence, R.I.," and the second, "Narrative of Inspector John R. Legrasse, 121 Bienville St., New Orleans, La., at 1908 A. A. S. Mtg.—Notes on Same, & Prof. Webb's Acct." The other manuscript papers were brief notes, some of them accounts of the queer dreams of different persons, some of them citations from theosophical books and magazines (notably W. Scott-Elliot's *Atlantis and the Lost Lemuria*), and the rest comments on long-surviving secret societies and hidden cults, with references to passages in such mythological and anthropological source-books as Frazer's *Golden Bough* and Miss Murray's *Witch-Cult in Western Europe*. The cuttings largely alluded to outré mental illness and outbreaks of group folly or mania in the spring of 1925.

The first half of the principal manuscript told a very particular tale. It appears that on March 1st, 1925, a thin, dark young man of neurotic and excited aspect had called upon Professor Angell bearing the singular clay bas-relief, which was then exceedingly damp and fresh. His card bore the name of Henry Anthony Wilcox, and my uncle had recognized him as the youngest son of an excellent family slightly known to him, who had latterly been studying sculpture at the Rhode Island School of Design and living alone at the Fleur-de-Lys Building near that institution. Wilcox was a precocious youth of known genius but great eccentricity, and had from childhood excited attention through the strange stories and odd dreams he was in the habit of relating. He called himself "psychically hypersensitive," but the staid folk of the ancient commercial city dismissed him as merely "queer." Never mingling much with his kind, he had dropped gradually from social visibility, and was now known only to a small group of aesthetes from other towns. Even the Providence Art Club, anxious to preserve its conservatism, had found him quite hopeless.

On the occasion of the visit, ran the professor's manuscript, the sculptor abruptly asked for the benefit of his host's archeological knowledge in identifying the hieroglyphics of the bas-relief. He spoke in a dreamy, stilted manner which suggested pose and alienated sympathy; and my uncle shewed some sharpness in replying, for the conspicuous freshness of the tablet implied kinship with anything but archeology. Young Wilcox's rejoinder, which impressed my uncle enough to make him recall and record it verbatim, was of a fantastically poetic cast which must have typified his whole conversation, and which I have since found highly characteristic of him. He said, "It is new, indeed, for I made it last night in a dream of strange cities; and dreams are older than brooding Tyre, or the contemplative Sphinx, or garden-girdled Babylon."

It was then that he began that rambling tale which suddenly played upon a sleeping memory and won the fevered interest of my uncle. There had been a slight earthquake tremor the night before, the most considerable felt in New England for some years; and Wilcox's imagination had been keenly affected. Upon retiring, he had had an unprecedented dream of great Cyclopean cities of titan blocks and sky-flung monoliths, all dripping with green ooze and sinister with latent horror. Hieroglyphics had covered the walls and pillars, and from some undetermined point below had come a voice that was not a voice; a chaotic sensation which only fancy could transmute into sound, but which he attempted to render by the almost unpronounceable jumble of letters, "*Cthulhu fhtagn.*"

This verbal jumble was the key to the recollection which excited and disturbed Professor Angell. He questioned the sculptor with scientific minuteness; and studied with frantic intensity the bas-relief on which the youth had found himself working, chilled and clad only in his night clothes, when waking had stolen bewilderingly over him. My uncle blamed his old age, Wilcox afterward said, for his slowness in recognizing both hieroglyphics and pictorial design. Many of his questions seemed highly out-of-place to his visitor, especially those which tried to connect the latter with strange cults or societies; and Wilcox could not understand the repeated promises of silence which he was offered in exchange for an admission of membership in some widespread mystical or paganly religious body. When Professor Angell became convinced that the sculptor was indeed ignorant of any cult or system of cryptic lore, he besieged his visitor with demands for future reports of dreams. This bore regular fruit, for after the first interview the manuscript records daily calls of the young man, during which he related startling fragments of nocturnal imaginery whose burden was always some terrible Cyclopean vista of dark and dripping stone, with a subterrene voice or intelligence shouting monotonously in enigmatical sense-impacts uninscribable save as gibberish. The two sounds frequently repeated are those rendered by the letters "*Cthulhu*" and "*R'lyeh.*"

On March 23d, the manuscript continued, Wilcox failed to appear; and inquiries at his quarters revealed that he had been stricken with an obscure sort of fever and taken to the home of his family in Waterman Street. He had cried out in the night, arousing several other artists in the building, and had manifested since then only alternations of unconsciousness and delirium. My uncle at once telephoned the family, and from that time forward kept close watch of the case; calling often at the Thayer Street office of Dr. Tobey, whom he learned to be in charge. The youth's febrile mind, apparently, was dwelling on strange things; and the doctor shuddered now and then as he spoke of them. They included not only a repetition of what he had formerly dreamed, but touched wildly on a gigantic thing "miles high" which walked or lumbered about. He at no time fully described this object but occasional frantic words, as repeated by Dr. Tobey, convinced the professor that it must be identical with the nameless monstrosity he had sought to depict in his dream-sculpture. Reference to this object, the doctor added, was invariably a prelude to the young man's subsidence into lethargy. His temperature, oddly enough, was not greatly above normal; but the whole condition was otherwise such as to suggest true fever rather than mental disorder.

On April 2nd at about 3 p.m. every trace of Wilcox's malady suddenly ceased. He sat upright in bed, astonished to find himself at home and completely ignorant of what had happened in dream or reality since the night of March 22nd. Pronounced well by his physician, he returned to his quarters in three days; but to Professor Angell he was of no further assistance. All traces of strange dreaming had vanished with his recovery, and my uncle kept no record of his night-thoughts after a week of pointless and irrelevant accounts of thoroughly usual visions.

Here the first part of the manuscript ended, but references to certain of the scattered notes gave me much material for thought—so much, in fact, that only the ingrained skepticism then forming my philosophy can account for my continued distrust of the artist. The notes in question were those descriptive of the dreams of various persons covering the same period as that in which young Wilcox had had his strange visitations. My uncle, it seems, had quickly instituted a prodigiously far-flung body of inquiries amongst nearly all the friends whom he could question without impertinence, asking for nightly reports of their dreams, and the dates of any notable visions for some time past. The reception of his request seems to have varied; but he must, at the very least, have received more responses than any ordinary man could have handled without a secretary. This original correspondence was not preserved, but his notes formed a thorough and really significant digest. Average people in society and business—New England's traditional "salt of the earth"—gave an almost completely negative result, though scattered cases of uneasy but formless nocturnal impressions appear here and there, always between March 23d and April 2nd—the period of young Wilcox's delirium. Scientific men were little more affected, though four cases of vague description suggest fugitive glimpses of strange landscapes, and in one case there is mentioned a dread of something abnormal.

It was from the artists and poets that the pertinent answers came, and I know that panic would have broken loose had they been able to compare notes. As it was, lacking their original letters, I half suspected the compiler of having asked leading questions, or of having edited the correspondence in corroboration of what he had latently resolved to see. That is why I continued to feel that Wilcox, somehow cognisant of the old data which my uncle had possessed, had been imposing on the veteran scientist. These responses from aesthetes told disturbing tale. From February 28th to April 2nd a large proportion of them had dreamed very bizarre things, the intensity of the dreams being immeasurably the stronger during the period of the sculptor's delirium. Over a fourth of those who reported anything, reported scenes and half-sounds not unlike those which Wilcox had described; and some of the dreamers confessed acute fear of the gigantic nameless thing visible toward the last. One case, which the note describes with emphasis, was very sad. The subject, a widely known architect with leanings toward theosophy and occultism, went violently insane on the date of young Wilcox's seizure, and expired several months later after incessant screamings to be saved from some escaped denizen of hell. Had my uncle referred to these cases by name instead of merely by number, I should have attempted some corroboration and personal investigation; but as it was, I succeeded in tracing down only a few. All of these, however, bore out the notes in full. I have often wondered if all the objects of the professor's questioning felt as puzzled as did this fraction. It is well that no explanation shall ever reach them.

The press cuttings, as I have intimated, touched on cases of panic, mania, and eccentricity during the given period. Professor Angell must have employed a cutting bureau, for the number of extracts was tremendous, and the sources scattered throughout the globe. Here was a nocturnal suicide in London, where a lone sleeper had leaped from a window after a shocking cry. Here likewise a rambling letter to the editor of a paper in South America, where a fanatic deduces a dire future from visions he has seen. A dispatch from California describes a theosophist colony as donning white robes en masse for some "glorious fulfillment" which never arrives, whilst items from India speak guardedly of serious native unrest toward the end of March. Voodoo orgies multiply in Hayti, and African outposts report ominous mutterings. American officers in the Philippines find certain tribes bothersome about this time, and New York policemen are mobbed by hysterical Levantines on the night of March 22-23. The west of Ireland, too, is full of wild rumour and legendry, and a fantastic painter named Ardois-Bonnot hangs a blasphemous "Dream Landscape" in the Paris spring salon of 1926. And so numerous are the recorded troubles in insane asylums that only a miracle can have stopped the medical fraternity from noting strange parallelisms and drawing mystified conclusions. A weird bunch of cuttings, all told; and I can at this date scarcely envisage the callous rationalism with which I set them aside. But I was then convinced that young Wilcox had known of the older matters mentioned by the professor.

II. THE TALE OF INSPECTOR LEGRASSE.

The older matters which had made the sculptor's dream and bas-relief so significant to my uncle formed the subject of the second half of his long manuscript. Once before, it appears, Professor Angell had seen the hellish outlines of the nameless monstrosity, puzzled over the unknown hieroglyphics, and heard the ominous syllables which can be rendered only as "*Cthulhu*"; and all this in so stirring and horrible a connexion that it is small wonder he pursued young Wilcox with queries and demands for data.

This earlier experience had come in 1908, seventeen years before, when the American Archaeological Society held its annual meeting in St. Louis. Professor Angell, as befitted one of his authority and attainments, had had a prominent part in all the deliberations; and was one of the first to be approached by the several outsiders who took advantage of the convocation to offer questions for correct answering and problems for expert solution.

The chief of these outsiders, and in a short time the focus of interest for the entire meeting, was a commonplace-looking middle-aged man who had travelled all the way from New Orleans for certain special information unobtainable from any local source. His name was John Raymond Legrasse, and he was by profession an Inspector of Police. With him he bore the subject of his visit, a grotesque, repulsive, and apparently very ancient stone statuette whose origin he was at a loss to determine. It must not be fancied that Inspector Legrasse had the least interest in archaeology. On the contrary, his wish for enlightenment was prompted by purely professional considerations. The statuette, idol, fetish, or whatever it was, had been captured some months before in the wooded swamps south of New Orleans during a raid on a supposed voodoo meeting; and so singular and hideous were the rites connected with it, that the police could not but realise that they had stumbled on a dark cult totally unknown to them, and infinitely more diabolic than even the blackest of the African voodoo circles. Of its origin, apart from the erratic and unbelievable tales extorted from the captured members, absolutely nothing was to be discovered; hence the anxiety of the police for any antiquarian lore which might help them to place the frightful symbol, and through it track down the cult to its fountain-head.

Inspector Legrasse was scarcely prepared for the sensation which his offering created. One sight of the thing had been enough to throw the assembled men of science into a state of tense excitement, and they lost no time in crowding around him to gaze at the diminutive figure whose utter strangeness and air of genuinely abysmal antiquity hinted so potently at unopened and archaic vistas. No recognised school of sculpture had animated this terrible object, yet centuries and even thousands of years seemed recorded in its dim and greenish surface of unplaceable stone.

The figure, which was finally passed slowly from man to man for close and careful study, was between seven and eight inches in height, and of exquisitely artistic workmanship. It represented a monster of vaguely anthropoid outline, but with an octopus-like head whose face was a mass of feelers, a scaly, rubbery-looking body, prodigious claws on hind and fore feet, and long, narrow wings behind. This thing, which seemed instinct with a fearsome and unnatural malignancy, was of a somewhat bloated corpulence, and squatted evilly on a rectangular block or pedestal covered with undecipherable characters. The tips of the wings touched the back edge of the block, the seat occupied the centre, whilst the long, curved claws of the doubled-up, crouching hind legs gripped the front edge and extended a quarter of the way down toward the bottom of the pedestal. The cephalopod head was bent forward, so that the ends of the facial feelers brushed the backs of huge fore paws which clasped the croucher's elevated knees. The aspect of the whole was abnormally life-like, and the more subtly fearful because its source was so totally unknown. Its vast, awesome, and incalculable age was unmistakable; yet not one link did it shew with any known type of art belonging to civilisation's youth—or indeed to any other time. Totally separate and apart, its very material was a mystery; for the soapy, greenish-black stone with its golden or iridescent flecks and striations resembled nothing familiar to geology or mineralogy. The characters along the base were equally baffling; and no member present, despite a representation of half the world's expert learning in this field, could form the least notion of even their remotest linguistic kinship. They, like the subject and material, belonged to something horribly remote and distinct from mankind as we know it. something frightfully suggestive of old and unhallowed cycles of life in which our world and our conceptions have no part.

And yet, as the members severally shook their heads and confessed defeat at the Inspector's problem, there was one man in that gathering who suspected a touch of bizarre familiarity in the monstrous shape and writing, and who presently told with some diffidence of the odd trifle he knew. This person was the late William Channing Webb, Professor of Anthropology in Princeton University, and an explorer of no slight note. Professor Webb had been engaged, forty-eight years before, in a tour of Greenland and Iceland in search of some Runic inscriptions which he failed to unearth; and whilst high up on the West Greenland coast had encountered a singular tribe or cult of degenerate Esquimaux whose religion, a curious form of devil-worship, chilled him with its deliberate bloodthirstiness and repulsiveness. It was a faith of which other Esquimaux knew little, and which they mentioned only with shudders, saying that it had come down from horribly ancient aeons before ever the world was made. Besides nameless rites and human sacrifices there were certain queer hereditary rituals addressed to a supreme elder devil or *tornasuk*; and of this Professor Webb had taken a careful phonetic copy from an aged *angekok* or wizard-priest, expressing the sounds in Roman letters as best he knew how. But just now of prime significance was the fetish which this cult had cherished, and around which they danced when the aurora leaped high over the ice cliffs. It was, the professor stated, a very crude bas-relief of stone, comprising a hideous picture and some cryptic writing. And so far as he could tell, it was a rough parallel in all essential features of the bestial thing now lying before the meeting.

This data, received with suspense and astonishment by the as-sembled members, proved doubly exciting to Inspector Legrasse; and he began at once to ply his informant with questions. Having noted and copied an oral ritual among the swamp cult-worship-pers his men had arrested, he besought the professor to remember as best he might the syllables taken down amongst the diabolist Esquimaux. There then followed an exhaustive comparison of details, and a moment of really awed silence when both detective and scientist agreed on the virtual identity of the phrase common to two hellish rituals so many worlds of distance apart. What, in substance, both the Esquimaux wizards and the Louisiana swamp-priests had chanted to their kindred idols was something very like this—the word-divisions being guessed at from traditional breaks in the phrase as chanted aloud:

"*Ph'nglui mglw'nafh Cthulhu R'lyeh wgah'nagl fhtagn.*"

Legrasse had one point in advance of Professor Webb, for several among his mongrel prisoners had repeated to him what older cel-ebrants had told them the words meant. This text, as given, ran something like this:

"*In his house at R'lyeh dead Cthulhu waits dreaming.*"

And now, in response to a general and urgent demand, Inspector Legrasse related as fully as possible his experience with the swamp worshippers; telling a story to which I could see my uncle attached profound significance. It savoured of the wildest dreams of myth-maker and theosophist, and disclosed an astonishing degree of cosmic imagination among such half-castes and pariahs as might be expected to possess it.

On November 1st, 1907, there had come to the New Orleans police a frantic summons from the swamp and lagoon country to the south. The squatters there, mostly primitive but good-natured descendants of Lafitte's men, were in the grip of stark terror from an unknown thing which had stolen upon them in the night. It was voodoo, apparently, but voodoo of a more terrible sort than they had ever known; and some of their women and children had disappeared since the malevolent tom-tom had begun its incessant beating far within the black haunted woods where no dweller ventured. There were insane shouts and harrowing screams, soul-chilling chants and dancing devil-flames; and, the frightened messenger added, the people could stand it no more.

So a body of twenty police, filling two carriages and an automobile, had set out in the late afternoon with the shivering squatter as a guide. At the end of the passable road they alighted, and for miles splashed on in silence through the terrible cypress woods where day never came. Ugly roots and malignant hanging nooses of Spanish moss beset them, and now and then a pile of dank stones or fragment of a rotting wall intensified by its hint of morbid habitation a depression which every malformed tree and every fungous islet combined to create. At length the squatter settlement, a miserable huddle of huts, hove in sight; and hysterical dwellers ran out to cluster around the group of bobbing lanterns. The muffled beat of tom-toms was now faintly audible far, far ahead; and a curdling shriek came at infrequent intervals when the wind shifted. A reddish glare, too, seemed to filter through pale undergrowth beyond the endless avenues of forest night. Reluctant even to be left alone again, each one of the cowed squatters refused point-blank to advance another inch toward the scene of unholy worship, so Inspector Legrasse and his nineteen colleagues plunged on unguided into black arcades of horror that none of them had ever trod before.

The region now entered by the police was one of traditionally evil repute, substantially unknown and untraversed by white men. There were legends of a hidden lake unglimpsed by mortal sight, in which dwelt a huge, formless white polypous thing with luminous eyes; and squatters whispered that bat-winged devils flew up out of caverns in inner earth to worship it at midnight. They said it had been there before d'Iberville, before La Salle, before the Indians, and before even the wholesome beasts and birds of the woods. It was nightmare itself, and to see it was to die. But it made men dream, and so they knew enough to keep away. The present voodoo orgy was, indeed, on the merest fringe of this abhorred area, but that location was bad enough; hence perhaps the very place of the worship had terrified the squatters more than the shocking sounds and incidents.

Only poetry or madness could do justice to the noises heard by Legrasse's men as they ploughed on through the black morass toward the red glare and muffled tom-toms. There are vocal qualities peculiar to men, and vocal qualities peculiar to beasts; and it is terrible to hear the one when the source should yield the other. Animal fury and orgiastic license here whipped themselves to daemoniac heights by howls and squawking ecstasies that tore and reverberated through those nighted woods like pestilential tempests from the gulfs of hell. Now and then the less organized ululation would cease, and from what seemed a well-drilled chorus of hoarse voices would rise in sing-song chant that hideous phrase or ritual:

"Ph'nglui mglw'nafh Cthulhu R'lyeh wgah'nagl fhtagn."
Then the men, having reached a spot where the trees were thinner, came suddenly in sight of the spectacle itself. Four of them reeled, one fainted, and two were shaken into a frantic cry which the mad cacophony of the orgy fortunately deadened. Legrasse dashed swamp water on the face of the fainting man, and all stood trembling and nearly hypnotised with horror.

In a natural glade of the swamp stood a grassy island of perhaps an acre's extent, clear of trees and tolerably dry. On this now leaped and twisted a more indescribable horde of human abnormality than any but a Sime or an Angarola could paint. Void of clothing, this hybrid spawn were braying, bellowing, and writhing about a monstrous ring-shaped bonfire; in the centre of which, revealed by occasional rifts in the curtain of flame, stood a great granite monolith some eight feet in height; on top of which, incongruous in its diminutiveness, rested the noxious carven statuette. From a wide circle of ten scaffolds set up at regular intervals with the flame-girt monolith as a centre hung, head downward, the oddly marred bodies of the helpless squatters who had disappeared. It was inside this circle that the ring of worshippers jumped and roared, the general direction of the mass motion being from left to right in endless Bacchanal between the ring of bodies and the ring of fire.

It may have been only imagination and it may have been only echoes which induced one of the men, an excitable Spaniard, to fancy he heard antiphonal responses to the ritual from some far and unillumined spot deeper within the wood of ancient legendry and horror. This man, Joseph D. Galvez, I later met and questioned; and he proved distractingly imaginative. He indeed went so far as to hint of the faint beating of great wings, and of a glimpse of shining eyes and a mountainous white bulk beyond the remotest trees—but I suppose he had been hearing too much native superstition.

Actually, the horrified pause of the men was of comparatively brief duration. Duty came first; and although there must have been nearly a hundred mongrel celebrants in the throng, the police relied on their firearms and plunged determinedly into the nauseous rout. For five minutes the resultant din and chaos were beyond description. Wild blows were struck, shots were fired, and escapes were made; but in the end Legrasse was able to count some forty-seven sullen prisoners, whom he forced to dress in haste and fall into line between two rows of policemen. Five of the worshippers lay dead, and two severely wounded ones were carried away on improvised stretchers by their fellow-prisoners. The image on the monolith, of course, was carefully removed and carried back by Legrasse.

Examined at headquarters after a trip of intense strain and weariness, the prisoners all proved to be men of a very low, mixed-blooded, and mentally aberrant type. Most were seamen, and a sprinkling of negroes and mulattoes, largely West Indians or Brava Portuguese from the Cape Verde Islands, gave a colouring of voodooism to the heterogeneous cult. But before many questions were asked, it became manifest that something far deeper and older than negro fetishism was involved. Degraded and ignorant as they were, the creatures held with surprising consistency to the central idea of their loathsome faith.

They worshipped, so they said, the Great Old Ones who lived ages before there were any men, and who came to the young world out of the sky. Those Old Ones were gone now, inside the earth and under the sea; but their dead bodies had told their secrets in dreams to the first men, who formed a cult which had never died. This was that cult, and the prisoners said it had always existed and always would exist, hidden in distant wastes and dark places all over the world until the time when the great priest Cthulhu, from his dark house in the mighty city of R'lyeh under the waters, should rise and bring the earth again beneath his sway. Some day he would call, when the stars were ready, and the secret cult would always be waiting to liberate him.

Meanwhile no more must be told. There was a secret which even torture could not extract. Mankind was not absolutely alone among the conscious things of earth, for shapes came out of the dark to visit the faithful few. But these were not the Great Old Ones. No man had ever seen the Old Ones. The carven idol was great Cthulhu, but none might say whether or not the others were precisely like him. No one could read the old writing now, but things were told by word of mouth. The chanted ritual was not the secret—that was never spoken aloud, only whispered. The chant meant only this: "In his house at R'lyeh dead Cthulhu waits dreaming."

Only two of the prisoners were found sane enough to be hanged, and the rest were committed to various institutions. All denied a part in the ritual murders, and averred that the killing had been done by Black Winged Ones which had come to them from their immemorial meeting-place in the haunted wood. But of those mysterious allies no coherent account could ever be gained. What the police did extract, came mainly from the immensely aged mestizo named Castro, who claimed to have sailed to strange ports and talked with undying leaders of the cult in the mountains of China.

Old Castro remembered bits of hideous legend that paled the speculations of theosophists and made man and the world seem recent and transient indeed. There had been aeons when other Things ruled on the earth, and They had had great cities. Remains of Them, he said the deathless Chinamen had told him, were still be found as Cyclopean stones on islands in the Pacific. They all died vast epochs of time before men came, but there were arts which could revive Them when the stars had come round again to the right positions in the cycle of eternity. They had, indeed, come themselves from the stars, and brought Their images with Them.

These Great Old Ones, Castro continued, were not composed altogether of flesh and blood. They had shape—for did not this star-fashioned image prove it?—but that shape was not made of matter. When the stars were right, They could plunge from world to world through the sky; but when the stars were wrong, They could not live. But although They no longer lived, They would never really die. They all lay in stone houses in Their great city of R'lyeh, preserved by the spells of mighty Cthulhu for a glorious resurrection when the stars and the earth might once more be ready for Them. But at that time some force from outside must serve to liberate Their bodies. The spells that preserved them intact likewise prevented Them from making an initial move, and They could only lie awake in the dark and think whilst uncounted millions of years rolled by. They knew all that was occurring in the universe, for Their mode of speech was transmitted thought. Even now They talked in Their tombs. When, after infinities of chaos, the first men came, the Great Old Ones spoke to the sensitive among them by moulding their dreams; for only thus could Their language reach the fleshly minds of mammals.

Then, whispered Castro, those first men formed the cult around tall idols which the Great Ones shewed them; idols brought in dim aeras from dark stars. That cult would never die till the stars came right again, and the secret priests would take great Cthulhu from His tomb to revive His subjects and resume His rule of earth. The time would be easy to know, for then mankind would have become as the Great Old Ones; free and wild and beyond good and evil, with laws and morals thrown aside and all men shouting and killing and revelling in joy. Then the liberated Old Ones would teach them new ways to shout and kill and revel and enjoy themselves, and all the earth would flame with a holocaust of ecstasy and freedom. Meanwhile the cult, by appropriate rites, must keep alive the memory of those ancient ways and shadow forth the prophecy of their return.

In the elder time chosen men had talked with the entombed Old Ones in dreams, but then something happened. The great stone city R'lyeh, with its monoliths and sepulchres, had sunk beneath the waves; and the deep waters, full of the one primal mystery through which not even thought can pass, had cut off the spectral intercourse. But memory never died, and the high-priests said that the city would rise again when the stars were right. Then came out of the earth the black spirits of earth, mouldy and shadowy, and full of dim rumours picked up in caverns beneath forgotten sea-bottoms. But of them old Castro dared not speak much. He cut himself off hurriedly, and no amount of persuasion or subtlety could elicit more in this direction. The size of the Old Ones, too, he curiously declined to mention. Of the cult, he said that he thought the centre lay amid the pathless desert of Arabia, where Irem, the City of Pillars, dreams hidden and untouched. It was not allied to the European witch-cult, and was virtually unknown beyond its members. No book had ever really hinted of it, though the deathless Chinamen said that there were double meanings in the *Necronomicon* of the mad Arab Abdul Al-Hazred which the initiated might read as they chose, especially the much-discussed couplet:

> *"That is not dead which can eternal lie,*
> *And with strange aeons even death may die."*

Legrasse, deeply impressed and not a little bewildered, had inquired in vain concerning the historic affiliations of the cult. Castro, apparently, had told the truth when he said that it was wholly secret. The authorities at Tulane University could shed no light upon either cult or image, and now the detective had come to the highest authorities in the country and met with no more than the Greenland tale of Professor Webb.

The feverish interest aroused at the meeting by Legrasse's tale, corroborated as it was by the statuette, is echoed in the subsequent correspondence of those who attended; although scant mention occurs in the formal publications of the society. Caution is the first care of those accustomed to face occasional charlatanry and imposture. Legrasse for some time lent the image to Professor Webb, but at the latter's death it was returned to him and remains in his possession, where I viewed it not long ago. It is truly a terrible thing, and unmistakably akin to the dream-sculpture of young Wilcox.

That my uncle was excited by the tale of the sculptor I did not wonder, for what thoughts must arise upon hearing, after a knowledge of what Legrasse had learned of the cult, of a sensitive young man who had *dreamed* not only the figure and exact hieroglyphics of the swamp-found image and the Greenland devil tablet, but had come *in his dreams* upon at least three of the precise words of the formula uttered alike by Esquimaux diabolists and mongrel Louisianans? Professor Angell's instant start on an investigation of the utmost thoroughness was eminently natural; though privately I suspected young Wilcox of having heard of the cult in some indirect way, and of having invented a series of dreams to heighten and continue the mystery at my uncle's expense. The dream-narratives and cuttings collected by the professor were, of course, strong corroboration; but the rationalism of my mind and the extravagance of the whole subject led me to adopt what I thought the most sensible conclusions. So, after thoroughly studying the manuscript again and correlating the theosophical and anthropological notes with the cult narrative of Legrasse, I made a trip to Providence to see the sculptor and give him the rebuke I thought proper for so boldly imposing upon a learned and aged man.

Wilcox still lived alone in the Fleur-de-Lys Building in Thomas Street, a hideous Victorian imitation of seventeenth-century Breton architecture which flaunts its stuccoed front amidst the lovely colonial houses on the ancient hill, and under the very shadow of the finest Georgian steeple in America. I found him at work in his rooms, and at once conceded from the specimens scattered about that his genius is indeed profound and authentic. He will, I believe, some time be heard from as one of the great decadents; for he has crystallised in clay and will one day mirror in marble those nightmares and phantasies which Arthur Machen evokes in prose, and Clark Ashton Smith makes visible in verse and in painting.

Dark, frail, and somewhat unkempt in aspect, he turned languidly at my knock and asked me my business without rising.

When I told him who I was, he displayed some interest; for my uncle had excited his curiosity in probing his strange dreams, yet had never explained the reason for the study. I did not enlarge his knowledge in this regard, but sought with some subtlety to draw him out. In a short time I became convinced of his absolute sincerity, for he spoke of the dreams in a manner none could mistake. They and their subconscious residuum had influenced his art profoundly, and he shewed me a morbid statue whose contours almost made me shake with the potency of its black suggestion. He could not recall having seen the original of this thing except in his own dream bas-relief, but the outlines had formed themselves insensibly under his hands. It was, no doubt, the giant shape he had raved of in delirium. That he really knew nothing of the hidden cult, save from what my uncle's relentless catechism had let fall, he soon made clear; and again I strove to think of some way in which he could possibly have received the weird impressions.

He talked of his dreams in a strangely poetic fashion; making me see with terrible vividness the damp Cyclopean city of slimy green stone—whose *geometry*, he oddly said, was *all wrong*—and hear with frightened expectancy the ceaseless, half-mental calling from underground: *"Cthulhu fhtagn,"* *"Cthulhu fhtagn."* These words had formed part of that dread ritual which told of dead Cthulhu's dream-vigil in his stone vault at R'lyeh, and I felt deeply moved despite my rational beliefs. Wilcox, I was sure, had heard of the cult in some casual way, and had soon forgotten it amidst the mass of his equally weird reading and imagining. Later, by virtue of its sheer impressiveness, it had found subconscious expression in dreams, in the bas-relief, and in the terrible statue I now beheld; so that his imposture upon my uncle had been a very innocent one. The youth was of a type, at once slightly affected and slightly ill-mannered, which I could never like, but I was willing enough now to admit both his genius and his honesty. I took leave of him amicably, and wish him all the success his talent promises.

The matter of the cult still remained to fascinate me, and at times I had visions of personal fame from researches into its origin and connexions. I visited New Orleans, talked with Legrasse and others of that old-time raiding-party, saw the frightful image, and even questioned such of the mongrel prisoners as still survived. Old Castro, unfortunately, had been dead for some years. What I now heard so graphically at first-hand, though it was really no more than a detailed confirmation of what my uncle had written, excited me afresh; for I felt sure that I was on the track of a very real, very secret, and very ancient religion whose discovery would make me an anthropologist of note. My attitude was still one of absolute materialism, *as I wish it still were*, and I discounted with almost inexplicable perversity the coincidence of the dream notes and odd cuttings collected by Professor Angell.

One thing I began to suspect, and which I now fear I *know,* is that my uncle's death was far from natural. He fell on a narrow hill street leading up from an ancient waterfront swarming with foreign mongrels, after a careless push from a negro sailor. I did not forget the mixed blood and marine pursuits of the cult-members in Louisiana, and would not be surprised to learn of secret methods and poison needles as ruthless and as anciently known as the cryptic rites and beliefs. Legrasse and his men, it is true, have been let alone; but in Norway a certain seaman who saw things is dead. Might not the deeper inquiries of my uncle after encountering the sculptor's data have come to sinister ears? I think Professor Angell died because he knew too much, or because he was likely to learn too much. Whether I shall go as he did remains to be seen, for I have learned much now.

III. THE MADNESS FROM THE SEA.

If heaven ever wishes to grant me a boon, it will be a total effacing of the results of a mere chance which fixed my eye on a certain stray piece of shelf-paper. It was nothing on which I would naturally have stumbled in the course of my daily round, for it was an old number of an Australian journal, the *Sydney Bulletin* for April 18, 1925. It had escaped even the cutting bureau which had at the time of its issuance been avidly collecting material for my uncle's research.

I had largely given over my inquiries into what Professor Angell called the "Cthulhu Cult," and was visiting a learned friend in Paterson, New Jersey; the curator of a local museum and a mineralogist of note. Examining one day the reserve specimens roughly set on the storage shelves in a rear room of the museum, my eye was caught by an odd picture in one of the old papers spread beneath the stones. It was the *Sydney Bulletin* I have mentioned, for my friend had wide affiliations in all conceivable foreign parts; and the picture was a half-tone cut of a hideous stone image almost identical with that which Legrasse had found in the swamp.

Eagerly clearing the sheet of its precious contents, I scanned the item in detail; and was disappointed to find it of only moderate length. What it suggested, however, was of portentous significance to my flagging quest; and I carefully tore it out for immediate action. It read as follows:

MYSTERY DERELICT FOUND AT SEA

Vigilant Arrives With Helpless Armed New Zealand Yacht in Tow.
One Survivor and Dead Man Found Aboard. Tale of
Desperate Battle and Deaths at Sea.
Rescued Seaman Refuses
Particulars of Strange Experience.
Odd Idol Found in His Possession. Inquiry
to Follow.

The Morrison Co.'s freighter *Vigilant,* bound from Valparaiso, arrived this morning at its wharf in Darling Harbour, having in tow the battled and disabled but heavily armed steam yacht *Alert* of Dunedin, N.Z., which was sighted April 12th in S. Latitude 34° 21', W. Longitude 152° 17' with one living and one dead man aboard.

The *Vigilant* left Valparaiso March 25th, and on April 2nd was driven considerably south of her course by exceptionally heavy storms and monster waves. On April 12th the derelict was sighted; and though apparently deserted, was found upon boarding to contain one survivor in a half-delirious condition and one man who had evidently been dead for more than a week. The living man was clutching a horrible stone idol of unknown origin, about a foot in height, regarding whose nature authorities at Sydney University, the Royal Society, and the Museum in College Street all profess complete bafflement, and which the survivor says he found in the cabin of the yacht, in a small carved shrine of common pattern.

This man, after recovering his senses, told an exceedingly strange story of piracy and slaughter. He is Gustaf Johansen, a Norwegian of some intelligence, and had been second mate of the two-masted schooner *Emma* of Auckland, which sailed for Callao February 20th with a complement of eleven men. The *Emma,* he says, was delayed and thrown widely south of her course by the great storm of March 1st, and on March 22nd, in S. Latitude 49° 51', W. Longitude 128° 34', encountered the *Alert,* manned by a queer and evil-looking crew of Kanakas and half-castes. Being ordered peremptorily to turn back, Capt. Collins refused; whereupon the strange crew began to fire savagely and without warning upon the schooner with a peculiarly heavy battery of brass cannon forming part of the yacht's equipment. The *Emma's* men shewed fight, says the survivor, and though the schooner began to sink from shots beneath the water-line they managed to heave alongside their enemy and board her, grappling with the savage crew on the yacht's deck, and being forced to kill them all, the number being slightly superior, because of their particularly abhorrent and desperate though rather clumsy mode of fighting.

Three of the *Emma's* men, including Capt. Collins and First Mate Green, were killed; and the remaining eight under Second Mate Johansen proceeded to navigate the captured yacht, going ahead in their original direction to see if any reason for their ordering back had existed. The next day, it appears, they raised and landed on a small island, although none is known to exist in that part of the ocean; and six of the men somehow died ashore, though Johansen is queerly reticent about this part of his story, and speaks only of their falling into a rock chasm. Later, it seems, he and one companion boarded the yacht and tried to manage her, but were beaten about by the storm of April 2nd. From that time till his rescue on the 12th the man remembers little, and he does not even recall when William Briden, his companion, died. Briden's death reveals no apparent cause, and was probably due to excitement or exposure. Cable advices from Dunedin report that the *Alert* was well known there as an island trader, and bore an evil reputation along the waterfront. It was owned by a curious group of half-castes whose frequent meetings and night trips to the woods attracted no little curiosity; and it had set sail in great haste just after the storm and earth tremors of March 1st. Our Auckland correspondent gives the *Emma* and her crew an excellent reputation, and Johansen is described as a sober and worthy man. The admiralty will institute an inquiry on the whole matter beginning tomorrow, at which every effort will be made to induce Johansen to speak more freely than he has done hitherto.

This was all, together with the picture of the hellish image; but what a train of ideas it started in my mind! Here were new treasuries of data on the Cthulhu Cult, and evidence that it had strange interests at sea as well as on land. What motive prompted the hybrid crew to order back the *Emma* as they sailed about with their hideous idol? What was the unknown island on which six of the *Emma's* crew had died, and about which the mate Johansen was so secretive? What had the vice-admiralty's investigation brought out, and what was known of the noxious cult in Dunedin? And most marvellous of all, what deep and more than natural linkage of dates was this which gave a malign and now undeniable significance to the various turns of events so carefully noted by my uncle?

March 1st—or February 28th according to the International Date Line—the earthquake and storm had come. From Dunedin the *Alert* and her noisome crew had darted eagerly forth as if imperiously summoned, and on the other side of the earth poets and artists had begun to dream of a strange, dank Cyclopean city whilst a young sculptor had moulded in his sleep the form of the dreaded Cthulhu. March 23d the crew of the *Emma* landed on an unknown island and left six men dead; and on that date the dreams of sensitive men assumed a heightened vividness and darkened with dread of a giant monster's malign pursuit, whilst an architect had gone mad and a sculptor had lapsed suddenly into delirium! And what of this storm of April 2nd—the date on which all dreams of the dank city ceased, and Wilcox emerged unharmed from the bondage of strange fever? What of all this—and of those hints of old Castro about the sunken, star-born Old Ones and their coming reign; their faithful cult *and their mastery of dreams?* Was I tottering on the brink of cosmic horrors beyond man's power to bear? If so, they must be horrors of the mind alone, for in some way the second of April had put a stop to whatever monstrous menace had begun its siege of mankind's soul.

That evening, after a day of hurried cabling and arranging, I bade my host adieu and took a train for San Francisco. In less than a month I was in Dunedin; where, however, I found that little was known of the strange cult-members who had lingered in the old sea-taverns. Waterfront scum was far too common for special mention; though there was vague talk about one inland trip these mongrels had made, during which faint drumming and red flame were noted on the distant hills. In Auckland I learned that Johansen had returned *with yellow hair turned white* after a perfunctory and inconclusive questioning at Sydney, and had thereafter sold his cottage in West Street and sailed with his wife to his old home in Oslo. Of his stirring experience he would tell his friends no more than he had told the admiralty officials, and all they could do was to give me his Oslo address.

After that I went to Sydney and talked profitlessly with seamen and members of the vice-admiralty court. I saw the *Alert,* now sold and in commercial use, at Circular Quay in Sydney Cove, but gained nothing from its non-committal bulk. The crouching image with its cuttlefish head, dragon body, scaly wings, and hiero-glyphed pedestal, was preserved in the Museum at Hyde Park; and I studied it long and well, finding it a thing of balefully exquisite workmanship, and with the same utter mystery, terrible antiquity, and unearthly strangeness of material which I had noted in Legrasse's smaller specimen. Geologists, the curator told me, had found it a monstrous puzzle; for they vowed that the world held no rock like it. Then I thought with a shudder of what old Castro had told Legrasse about the primal Great Ones: "They had come from the stars, and had brought Their images with Them."

Shaken with such a mental revolution as I had never before known, I now resolved to visit Mate Johansen in Oslo. Sailing for London, I reëmbarked at once for the Norwegian capital; and one autumn day landed at the trim wharves in the shadow of the Egeberg. Johansen's address, I discovered, lay in the Old Town of King Harold Haardrada, which kept alive the name of Oslo dur-ing all the centuries that the greater city masqueraded as "Christiana." I made the brief trip by taxicab, and knocked with palpitant heart at the door of a neat and ancient building with plastered front. A sad-faced woman in black answered my sum-mons, and I was stung with disappointment when she told me in halting English that Gustaf Johansen was no more.

He had not long survived his return, said his wife, for the

doings at sea in 1925 had broken him. He had told her no more than he told the public, but had left a long manuscript—of "technical matters" as he said—written in English, evidently in order to guard her from the peril of casual perusal. During a walk through a narrow lane near the Gothenburg dock, a bundle of papers falling from an attic window had knocked him down. Two Lascar sailors at once helped him to his feet, but before the ambulance could reach him he was dead. Physicians found no adequate cause for the end, and laid it to heart trouble and a weakened constitution.

I now felt gnawing at my vitals that dark terror which will never leave me till I, too, am at rest; "accidentally" or otherwise. Persuading the widow that my connexion with her husband's "technical matters" was sufficient to entitle me to his manuscript, I bore the document away and began to read it on the London boat. It was a simple, rambling thing—a naive sailor's effort at a post-facto diary—and strove to recall day by day that last awful voyage. I cannot attempt to transcribe it verbatim in all its cloudiness and redundance, but I will tell its gist enough to shew why the sound the water against the vessel's sides became so unendurable to me that I stopped my ears with cotton.

Johansen, thank God, did not know quite all, even though he saw the city and the Thing, but I shall never sleep calmly again when I think of the horrors that lurk ceaselessly behind life in time and in space, and of those unhallowed blasphemies from elder stars which dream beneath the sea, known and favoured by a nightmare cult ready and eager to loose them upon the world whenever another earthquake shall heave their monstrous stone city again to the sun and air.

Johansen's voyage had begun just as he told it to the vice-admiralty. The *Emma*, in ballast, had cleared Auckland on February 20th, and had felt the full force of that earthquake-born tempest which must have heaved up from the sea-bottom the horrors that filled men's dreams. Once more under control, the ship was making good progress when held up by the *Alert* on March 22nd, and I could feel the mate's regret as he wrote of her bombardment and sinking. Of the swarthy cult-fiends on the *Alert* he speaks with significant horror. There was some peculiarly abominable quality about them which made their destruction seem almost a duty, and Johansen shews ingenuous wonder at the charge of ruthlessness brought against his party during the proceedings of the court of inquiry. Then, driven ahead by curiosity in their captured yacht under Johansen's command, the men sight a great stone pillar sticking out of the sea, and in S. Latitude 47° 9', W. Longitude 126° 43', come upon a coastline of mingled mud, ooze, and weedy Cyclopean masonry which can be nothing less than the tangible substance of earth's supreme terror—the nightmare corpse-city of R'lyeh, that was built in measureless aeons behind history by the vast, loathsome shapes that seeped down from the dark stars. There lay great Cthulhu and his hordes, hidden in green slimy vaults and sending out at last, after cycles incalculable, the thoughts that spread fear to the dreams of the sensitive and called imperiously to the faithful to come on a pilgrimage of liberation and restoration. All this Johansen did not suspect, but God knows he soon saw enough!

I suppose that only a single mountain-top, the hideous monolith-crowned citadel whereon great Cthulhu was buried, actually emerged from the waters. When I think of the *extent* of all that may be brooding down there I almost wish to kill myself forthwith. Johansen and his men were awed by the cosmic majesty of this dripping Babylon of elder daemons, and must have guessed without guidance that it was nothing of this or of any sane planet. Awe at the unbelievable size of the greenish stone blocks, at the dizzying height of the great carven monolith, and at the stupefying identity of the colossal statues and bas-reliefs with the queer image found in the shrine on the *Alert,* is poignantly visible in every line of the mates frightened description.

Without knowing what futurism is like, Johansen achieved

something very close to it when he spoke of the city; for instead of describing any definite structure or building, he dwells only on broad impressions of vast angles and stone surfaces—surfaces too great to belong to anything right or proper for this earth, and impious with horrible images and hieroglyphs. I mention his talk about *angles* because it suggests something Wilcox had told me of his awful dreams. He said that the *geometry* of the dream-place he saw was abnormal, non-Euclidean, and loathsomely redolent of spheres and dimensions apart from ours. Now an unlettered seaman felt the same thing whilst gazing at the terrible reality.

Johansen and his men landed at a sloping mud-bank on this monstrous Acropolis, and clambered slipperily up over titan oozy blocks which could have been no mortal staircase. The very sun of heaven seemed distorted when viewed through the polarising miasma welling out from this sea-soaked perversion, and twisted menace and suspense lurked leeringly in those crazily elusive angles of carven rock where a second glance shewed concavity after the first shewed convexity.

Something very like fright had come over all the explorers before anything more definite than rock and ooze and weed was seen. Each would have fled had he not feared the scorn of the others, and it was only half-heartedly that they searched—vainly, as it proved—for some portable souvenir to bear away.

It was Rodriguez the Portuguese who climbed up the foot of the monolith and shouted of what he had found. The rest followed him, and looked curiously at the immense carved door with the now familiar squid-dragon bas-relief. It was, Johansen said, like a great barn-door; and they all felt that it was a door because of the ornate lintel, threshold, and jambs around it, though they could not decide whether it lay flat like a trap-door or slantwise like an outside cellar-door. As Wilcox would have said, the geometry of the place was all wrong. One could not be sure that the sea and the ground were horizontal, hence the relative position of everything else seemed phantasmally variable.

Briden pushed at the stone in several places without result. Then Donovan felt over it delicately around the edge, pressing each point separately as he went. He climbed interminably along the grotesque stone moulding—that is, one would call it climbing if the thing was not after all horizontal—and the men wondered how any door in the universe could be so vast. Then, very softly and slowly, the acre-great lintel began to give inward at the top; and they saw that it was balanced. Donovan slid or somehow propelled himself down or along the jamb and rejoined his fellows, and everyone watched the queer recession of the monstrously carven portal. In this phantasy of prismatic distortion it moved anomalously in a diagonal way, so that all the rules of matter and perspective seemed upset.

The aperture was black with a darkness almost material. That tenebrousness was indeed a *positive quality*; for it obscured such parts of the inner walls as ought to have been revealed, and actually burst forth like smoke from its aeon-long imprisonment, visibly darkening the sun as it slunk away into the shrunken and gibbous sky on flapping membranous wings. The odour arising from the newly opened depths was intolerable, and at length the quick-eared Hawkins thought he heard a nasty, slopping sound down there. Everyone listened, and everyone was listening still when It lumbered slobberingly into sight and gropingly squeezed Its gelatinous green immensity through the black doorway into the tainted outside air of that poison city of madness.

Poor Johansen's handwriting almost gave out when he wrote of this. Of the six men who never reached the ship, he thinks two perished of pure fright in that accursed instant. The Thing cannot be described—there is no language for such abysms of shrieking and immemorial lunacy, such eldritch contradictions of all matter, force, and cosmic order. A mountain walked or stumbled. God! What wonder that across the earth a great architect went mad, and poor Wilcox raved with fever in that telepathic instant? The Thing of the idols, the green, sticky spawn of the stars, had awaked to claim his own. The stars were right again, and what an age-old cult had failed to do by design, a band of innocent sailors had done by accident. After vigintillions of years great Cthulhu was loose again, and ravening for delight.

Three men were swept up by the flabby claws before anybody turned. God rest them, if there be any rest in the universe. They were Donovan, Guerrera, and Ångstrom. Parker slipped as the other three were plunging frenziedly over endless vistas of green-crusted rock to the boat, and Johansen swears he was swallowed up by an angle of masonry which shouldn't have been there; an angle which was acute, but behaved as if it were obtuse. So only Briden and Johansen reached the boat, and pulled desperately for the *Alert* as the mountainous monstrosity flopped down the slimy stones and hesitated, floundering at the edge of the water.

Steam had not been suffered to go down entirely, despite the departure of all hands for the shore; and it was the work of only a few moments of feverish rushing up and down between wheel and engines to get the *Alert* under way. Slowly, amidst the distorted horrors of that indescribable scene, she began to churn the lethal waters; whilst on the masonry of that charnel shore that was not of earth the titan Thing from the stars slavered and gibbered like Polypheme cursing the fleeing ship of Odysseus. Then, bolder than the storied Cyclops, great Cthulhu slid greasily into the water and began to pursue with vast wave-raising strokes of cosmic potency. Briden looked back and went mad, laughing shrilly as he kept on laughing at intervals till death found him one night in the cabin whilst Johansen was wandering deliriously.

But Johansen had not given out yet. Knowing that the Thing could surely overtake the *Alert* until steam was fully up, he resolved on a desperate chance; and, setting the engine for full speed, ran lightning-like on deck and reversed the wheel. There was a mighty eddying and foaming in the noisome brine, and as the steam mounted higher and higher the brave Norwegian drove his vessel head on against the pursuing jelly which rose above the unclean froth like the stern of a daemon galleon. The awful squid-head with writhing feelers came nearly up to the bowsprit of the sturdy yacht, but Johansen drove on relentlessly. There was a bursting as of an exploding bladder, a slushy nastiness as of a cloven sunfish, a stench as of a thousand opened graves, and a sound that the chronicler could not put on paper. For an instant the ship was befouled by an acrid and blinding green cloud, and then there was only a venomous seething astern; where—God in heaven!—the scattered plasticity of that nameless sky-spawn was nebulously *recombining* in its hateful original form, whilst its distance widened every second as the *Alert* gained impetus from its mounting steam.

That was all. After that Johansen only brooded over the idol in the cabin and attended to a few matters of food for himself and the laughing maniac by his side. He did not try to navigate after the first bold flight, for the reaction had taken something out of his soul. Then came the storm of April 2nd, and a gathering of the clouds about his consciousness. There is a sense of spectral whirling through liquid gulfs of infinity, of dizzying rides through reeling universes on a comet's tail, and of hysterical plunges from the pit to the moon and from the moon back again to the pit, all livened by a cachinnating chorus of the distorted, hilarious elder gods and the green, bat-winged mocking imps of Tartarus.

Out of that dream came rescue—the *Vigilant*, the vice-admiralty court, the streets of Dunedin, and the long voyage back home to the old house by the Egeberg. He could not tell—they would think him mad. He would write of what he knew before death came, but his wife must not guess. Death would be a boon if only it could blot out the memories.

That was the document I read, and now I have placed it in the tin box beside the bas-relief and the papers of Professor Angell.

With it shall go this record of mine—this test of my own sanity, wherein is pieced together that which I hope may never be pieced together again. I have looked upon all that the universe has to hold of horror, and even the skies of spring and the flowers of summer must ever afterward be poison to me. But I do not think my life will be long. As my uncle went, as poor Johansen went, so I shall go. I know too much, and the cult still lives.

Cthulhu still lives, too, I suppose, again in that chasm of stone which has shielded him since the sun was young. His accursed city is sunken once more, for the *Vigilant* sailed over the spot after the April storm; but his ministers on earth still bellow and prance and slay around idol-capped monoliths in lonely places. He must have been trapped by the sinking whilst within his black abyss, or the world would by now be screaming with fright and frenzy. Who knows the end? What has risen may sink, and what has sunk may rise. Loathsomeness waits and dreams in the deep, and decay spreads over the tottering cities of men. A time will come—but I must not and cannot think! Let me pray that, if I do not survive this manuscript, my executors may put caution before audacity and see that it meets no other eye.

THE WHISPERER IN DARKNESS

(1931)

by H. P. LOVECRAFT

I.

Bear in mind closely that I did not see any actual visual horror at the end. To say that a mental shock was the cause of what I inferred—that last straw which sent me racing out of the lonely Akeley farmhouse and through the wild domed hills of Vermont in a commandeered motor at night—is to ignore the plainest facts of my final experience. Notwithstanding the deep extent to which I shared the information and speculations of Henry Akely, the things I saw and heard, and the admitted vividness the impression produced on me by these things, I cannot prove even now whether I was right or wrong in my hideous inference. For after all Akeley's disappearance establishes nothing. People found nothing amiss in his house despite the bullet-marks on the outside and inside. It was just as though he had walked out casually for a ramble in the hills and failed to return. There was not even a sign that a guest had been there, or that those horrible cylinders and machines had been stored in the study. That he had mortally feared the crowded green hills and endless trickle of brooks among which he had been born and reared, means nothing at all, either; for thousands are subject to just such morbid fears. Eccentricity, moreover, could easily account for his strange acts and apprehensions toward the last.

The whole matter began, so far as I am concerned, with the historic and unprecedented Vermont floods of November 3, 1927. I was then, as now, an instructor of literature at Miskatonic University in Arkham, Massachusetts, and an enthusiastic amateur student of New England folklore. Shortly after the flood, amidst the varied reports of hardship, suffering, and organized relief which filled the press, there appeared certain odd stories of things found floating in some of the swollen rivers; so that many of my friends embarked on curious discussions and appealed to me to shed what light I could on the subject. I felt flattered at having my folklore study taken so seriously, and did what I could to belittle the wild, vague tales which seemed so clearly an outgrowth of old rustic superstitions. It amused me to find several persons of education who insisted that some stratum of obscure, distorted fact might underlie the rumors.

The tales thus brought to my notice came mostly through newspaper cuttings; though one yarn had an oral source and was repeated to a friend of mine in a letter from his mother in Hardwick, Vermont. The type of thing described was essentially the same in all cases, though there seemed to be three separate instances involved—one connected with the Winooski River near Montpelier, another attached to the West River in Windham County beyond Newfane, and a third centering in the Passumpsic in Caledonia County above Lyndonville. Of course many of the stray items mentioned other instances, but on analysis they all seemed to boil down to these three. In each case country folk reported seeing one or more very bizarre and disturbing objects in the surging waters that poured down from the unfrequented hills, and there was a widespread tendency to connect these sights with a primitive, half-forgotten cycle of whispered legend which old people resurrected for the occasion.

What people thought they saw were organic shapes not quite like any they had ever seen before. Naturally, there were many human bodies washed along by the streams in that tragic period; but those who described these strange shapes felt quite sure that they were not human, despite some superficial resemblances in size and general outline. Nor, said the witnesses, could they have been any kind of animal known to Vermont. They were pinkish things about five feet long; with crustaceous bodies bearing vast pairs of dorsal fins or membranous wings and several sets of articulated limbs, and with a sort of convoluted ellipsoid, covered with multitudes of very short antennae, where a head would ordinarily be. It was really remarkable how closely the reports from different sources tended to coincide; though the wonder was lessened by the fact that the old legends, shared at one time throughout the hill country, furnished a morbidly vivid picture which might well have coloured the imaginations of all the witnesses concerned. It was my conclusion that such witnesses—in every case naive and simple backwoods folk—had glimpsed the battered and bloated bodies of human beings or farm animals in the whirling currents; and had allowed the half-remembered folklore to invest these pitiful objects with fantastic attributes.

The ancient folklore, while cloudy, evasive, and largely forgotten by the present generation, was of a highly singular character, and obviously reflected the influence of still earlier Indian tales. I knew it well, though I had never been in Vermont, through the exceedingly rare monograph of Eli Davenport, which embraces material orally obtained prior to 1839 among the oldest people of the state. This material, moreover, closely coincided with tales which I had personally heard from elderly rustics in the mountains of New Hampshire. Briefly summarized, it hinted at a hidden race of monstrous beings which lurked somewhere among the remoter hills—in the deep woods of the highest peaks, and the dark valleys where streams trickle from unknown sources. These beings were seldom glimpsed, but evidences of their presence were reported by those who had ventured farther than usual up the slopes of certain mountains or into certain deep, steep-sided gorges that even the wolves shunned.

There were queer footprints or claw-prints in the mud of brook-margins and barren patches, and curious circles of stones, with the grass around them worn away, which did not seem to have been placed or entirely shaped by Nature. There were, too, certain caves of problematical depth in the sides of the hills; with mouths closed by boulders in a manner scarcely accidental, and with more than an average quota of the queer prints leading both toward and away from them—if indeed the direction of these prints could be justly estimated. And worst of all, there were the things which adventurous people had seen very rarely in the twi-light of the remotest valleys and the dense perpendicular woods above the limits of normal hill-climbing.

It would have been less uncomfortable if the stray accounts of these things had not agreed so well. As it was, nearly all the rumors had several points in common; averring that the creatures were a sort of huge, light-red crab with many pairs of legs and with two great bat-like wings in the middle of the back. They sometimes walked on all their legs, and sometimes on the hindmost pair only, using the others to convey large objects of indeterminate nature. On one occasion they were spied in considerable numbers, a detachment of them wading along a shallow woodland water-course three abreast in evidently disciplined formation. Once a specimen was seen flying—launching itself from the top of a bald, lonely hill at night and vanishing in the sky after its great flapping wings had been silhouetted an instant against the full moon.

These things seemed content, on the whole, to let mankind

alone; though they were at times held responsible for the disappearance of venturesome individuals—especially persons who built houses too close to certain valleys or too high up on certain mountains. Many localities came to be known as inadvisable to settle in, the feeling persisting long after the cause was forgotten. People would look up at some of the neighbouring mountain-precipices with a shudder, even when not recalling how many settlers had been lost, and how many farmhouses burnt to ashes, on the lower slopes of those grim, green sentinels.

But while according to the earliest legends the creatures would appear to have harmed only those trespassing on their privacy; there were later accounts of their curiosity respecting men, and of their attempts to establish secret outposts in the human world. There were tales of the queer claw-prints seen around farmhouse windows in the morning, and of occasional disappearances in regions outside the obviously haunted areas. Tales, besides, of buzzing voices in imitation of human speech which made surprising offers to lone travelers on roads and cart-paths in the deep woods, and of children frightened out of their wits by things seen or heard where the primal forest pressed close upon their dooryards. In the final layer of legends—the layer just preceding the decline of superstition and the abandonment of close contact with the dreaded places—there are shocked references to hermits and remote farmers who at some period of life appeared to have undergone a repellent mental change, and who were shunned and whispered about as mortals who had sold themselves to the strange beings. In one of the northeastern counties it seemed to be a fashion about 1800 to accuse eccentric and unpopular recluses of being allies or representatives of the abhorred things.

As to what the things were—explanations naturally varied. The common name applied to them was "those ones," or "the old ones," though other terms had a local and transient use. Perhaps the bulk of the Puritan settlers set them down bluntly as familiars of the devil, and made them a basis of awed theological speculation. Those with Celtic legendry in their heritage—mainly the Scotch-Irish element of New Hampshire, and their kindred who had settled in Vermont on Governor Wentworth's colonial grants—linked them vaguely with the malign fairies and "little people" of the bogs and raths, and protected themselves with scraps of incantation handed down through many generations. But the Indians had the most fantastic theories of all. While different tribal legends differed, there was a marked consensus of belief in certain vital particulars; it being unanimously agreed that the creatures were not native to this earth.

The Pennacook myths, which were the most consistent and picturesque, taught that the Winged Ones came from the Great Bear in the sky, and had mines in our earthly hills whence they took a kind of stone they could not get on any other world. They did not live here, said the myths, but merely maintained outposts and flew back with vast cargoes of stone to their own stars in the north. They harmed only those earth-people who got too near them or spied upon them. Animals shunned them through instinctive hatred, not because of being hunted. They could not eat the things and animals of earth, but brought their own food from the stars. It was bad to get near them, and sometimes young hunters who went into their hills never came back. It was not good, either, to listen to what they whispered at night in the forest with voices like a bee's that tried to be like the voices of men. They knew the speech of all kinds of men—Pennacooks, Hurons, men of the Five Nations—but did not seem to have or need any speech of their own. They talked with their heads, which changed colour in different ways to mean different things.

All the legendry, of course, white and Indian alike, died down during the nineteenth century, except for occasional atavistical flareups. The ways of the Vermonters became settled; and once their habitual paths and dwellings were established according to a certain fixed plan, they remembered less and less what fears and avoidances had determined that plan, and even that there had been any fears or avoidances. Most people simply knew that certain hilly regions were considered as highly unhealthy, unprofitable, and generally unlucky to live in, and that the farther one kept from them the better off one usually was. In time the ruts of custom and economic interest became so deeply cut in approved places that there was no longer any reason for going outside them, and the haunted hills were left deserted by accident rather than by design. Save during infrequent local scares, only wonder-loving grand-mothers and retrospective nonagenarians ever whispered of beings dwelling in those hills; and even such whispers admitted that there was not much to fear from those things now that they were used to the presence of houses and settlements, and now that human beings let their chosen territory severely alone.

All this I had long known from my reading, and from certain folk tales picked up in New Hampshire; hence when the flood-time rumours began to appear, I could easily guess what imagina-tive background had evolved them. I took great pains to explain this to my friends, and was correspondingly amused when several contentious souls continued to insist on a possible element of truth in the reports. Such persons tried to point out that the early legends had a significant persistence and uniformity, and that the virtually unexplored nature of the Vermont hills made it unwise to be dogmatic about what might or might not dwell among them; nor could they be silenced by my assurance that all the myths were of a well-known pattern common to most of mankind and deter-mined by early phases of imaginative experience which always produced the same type of delusion.

It was of no use to demonstrate to such opponents that the Vermont myths differed but little in essence from those universal legends of natural personification which filled the ancient world with fauns and dryads and satyrs, suggested the *kallikanzari* of modern Greece, and gave to wild Wales and Ireland their dark hints of strange, small, and terrible hidden races of troglodytes and burrowers. No use, either, to point out the even more startlingly similar belief of the Nepalese hill tribes in the dreaded *Mi-Go* or "Abominable Snow-Men" who lurk hideously amidst the ice and rock pinnacles of the Himalayan summits. When I brought up this evidence, my opponents turned it against me by claiming that it must imply some actual historicity for the ancient tales; that it must argue the real existence of some queer elder earth-race, driven to hiding after the advent and dominance of mankind, which might very conceivably have survived in reduced numbers to relatively recent times—or even to the present.

The more I laughed at such theories, the more these stubborn friends asseverated them; adding that even without the heritage of legend the recent reports were too clear, consistent, detailed, and sanely prosaic in manner of telling, to be completely ignored. Two or three fanatical extremists went so far as to hint at possible meanings in the ancient Indian tales which gave the hidden beings a nonterrestrial origin; citing the extravagant books of Charles Fort with their claims that voyagers from other worlds and outer space have often visited the earth. Most of my foes, however, were merely romanticists who insisted on trying to transfer to real life the fantastic lore of lurking "little people" made popular by the magnificent horror-fiction of Arthur Machen.

II.

As was only natural under the circumstances, this piquant debating finally got into print in the form of letters to the *Arkham Advertiser;* some of which were copied in the press of those Vermont regions whence the flood-stories came. The *Rutland Herald* gave half a page of extracts from the letters on both sides, while the *Brattleboro Reformer* reprinted one of my long historical and mythological summaries in full, with some accompanying comments in "The Pendrifter's" thoughtful column which supported and applauded my skeptical conclusions. By the spring of 1928 I was almost a well-known figure in Vermont, notwithstanding the fact that I had never set foot in the state. Then came the challenging letters from Henry Akeley which impressed me so profoundly, and which took me for the first and last time to that fascinating realm of crowded green precipices and muttering forest streams.

Most of what I know of Henry Wentworth Akeley was gathered by correspondence with his neighbours, and with his only son in California, after my experience in his lonely farmhouse. He was, I discovered, the last representative on his home soil of a long, locally distinguished line of jurists, administrators, and gentlemen-agriculturists. In him, however, the family mentally had veered away from practical affairs to pure scholarship; so that he had been a notable student of mathematics, astronomy, biology, anthropology, and folklore at the University of Vermont. I had never previously heard of him, and he did not give many autobiographical details in his communications; but from the first I saw he was a man of character, education, and intelligence, albeit a recluse with very little worldly sophistication.

Despite the incredible nature of what he claimed, I could not help at once taking Akeley more seriously than I had taken any of the other challengers of my views. For one thing, he was really close to the actual phenomena—visible and tangible—that he speculated so grotesquely about; and for another thing, he was amazingly willing to leave his conclusions in a tentative state like a true man of science. He had no personal preferences to advance, and was always guided by what he took to be solid evidence. Of course I began by considering him mistaken, but gave him credit for being intelligently mistaken; and at no time did I emulate some of his friends in attributing his ideas, and his fear of the lonely green hills, to insanity. I could see that there was a great deal to the man, and knew that what he reported must surely come from strange circumstance deserving investigation, however little it might have to do with the fantastic causes he assigned. Later on I received from him certain material proofs which placed the matter on a somewhat different and bewilderingly bizarre basis.

I cannot do better than transcribe in full, so far as is possible, the long letter in which Akeley introduced himself, and which formed such an important landmark in my own intellectual history. It is no longer in my possession, but my memory holds almost every word of its portentous message; and again I affirm my confidence in the sanity of the man who wrote it. Here is the text—a text which reached me in the cramped, archaic-looking scrawl of one who had obviously not mingled much with the world during his sedate, scholarly life.

> R.F.D. #2,
> Townshend, Windham Co.,
> Vermont.
> May 5, 1928.

Albert N. Wilmarth, Esq.,
118 Saltonstall St.,
Arkham, Mass.

My dear Sir:—

I have read with great interest the *Brattleboro Reformer's* reprint (Apr. 23, '28) of your letter on the recent stories of strange bodies seen floating in our flooded streams last fall, and on the curious folklore they so well agree with. It is easy to see why an outlander would take the position you take, and even why "Pendrifter" agrees with you. That is the attitude generally taken by educated persons both in and out of Vermont, and was my own attitude as a young man (I am now 57) before my studies, both general and in Davenport's book, led me to do some exploring in parts of the hills hereabouts not usually visited.

I was directed toward such studies by the queer old tales I used to hear from elderly farmers of the more ignorant sort, but now I wish I had let the whole matter alone. I might say, with all proper modesty, that the subject of anthropology and folklore is by no means strange to me. I took a good deal of it at college, and am familiar with most of the standard authorities such as Tylor, Lubbock, Frazer, Quatrefages, Murray, Osborn, Keith, Boule, G. Elliott Smith, and so on. It is no news to me that tales of hidden races are as old as all mankind. I have seen the reprints of letters from you, and those agreeing with you, in the *Rutland Herald,* and guess I know about where your controversy stands at the present time.

What I desire to say now is, that I am afraid your adversaries are nearer right than yourself, even though all reason seems to be on your side. They are nearer right than they realise themselves—for of course they go only by theory, and cannot know what I know. If I knew as little of the matter as they, I would feel justified in believing as they do. I would be wholly on your side.

You can see that I am having a hard time getting to the point, probably because I really dread getting to the point; but the upshot of the matter is that *I have certain evidence that monstrous things do indeed live in the woods on the high hills which nobody visits.* I have not seen any of the things floating in the rivers, as reported, *but I have seen things like them* under circumstances I dread to repeat. I have seen footprints, and of late have seen them nearer my own home (I live in the old Akeley place south of Townshend Village, on the side of Dark Mountain) than I dare tell you now. And I have overheard voices in the woods at certain points that I will not even begin to describe on paper.

At one place I heard them so much that I took a phonograph there—with a dictaphone attachment and wax blank—and I shall try to arrange to have you hear the record I got. I have run it on the machine for some of the old people up here, and one of the voices had nearly scared them paralysed by reason of its likeness to a certain voice (that buzzing voice in the woods which Davenport mentions) that their grandmothers have told about and mimicked for them. I know what most people think of a man who tells about "hearing voices"—but before you draw conclusions just listen to this record and ask some of the older backwoods people what they think of it. If you can account for it normally, very well; but there must be something behind it. *Ex nihilo nihil fit,* you know.

Now my object in writing you is not to start an argument but to give you information which I think a man of your tastes will find deeply interesting. *This is private. Publicly I am on your side,* for certain things shew me that it does not do for people to know too much about these matters. My own studies are now wholly private, and I would not think of saying anything to attract people's attention and cause them to visit the places I have explored. It is true—terribly true—*that there are non-human creatures watching us all the time;* with spies among us gathering information. It is from a wretched man who, if he was sane (as I think he was) *was one of those spies,* that I got a large part of my clues to the matter. He later killed himself, but I have reason to think there are others now.

The things come from another planet, being able to live in interstellar space and fly through it on clumsy, powerful wings which have a way of resisting the aether but which are too poor at steering to be of much use in helping them about on earth. I will tell you about this later if you do not dismiss me at once as a madman. They come here to get metals from mines that go deep under the hills, *and I think I know where they come from.* They will not hurt us if we let them alone, but no one can say what will happen if we get too curious about them. Of course a good army of men could wipe out their mining colony. That is what they are afraid of. But if that happened, more would come from *outside*—any number of them. They could easily conquer the earth, but have not tried so far because they have not needed to. They would rather leave things as they are to save bother.

I think they mean to get rid of me because of what I have discovered. There is a great black stone with unknown hieroglyphics half worn away which I found in the woods on Round Hill, east of here; and after I took it home everything became different. If they think I suspect too much they will either kill me *or take me off the earth to where they come from.* They like to take away men of learning once in a while, to keep informed on the state of things in the human world.

This leads me to my secondary purpose in addressing you—namely, to urge you to hush up the present debate rather than give it more publicity. *People must be kept away from these hills,* and in order to effect this, their curiosity ought not to be aroused any further. Heaven knows there is peril enough anyway, with promoters and real estate men flooding Vermont with herds of summer people to over-run the wild places and cover the hills with cheap bungalows.

I shall welcome further communication with you, and shall try to send you that phonograph record and black stone (which is so worn that photographs don't shew much) by express if you are willing. I say "try" because I think those creatures have a way of tampering with things around here. There is a sullen furtive fellow named Brown, on a farm near the village, who I think is their spy. Little by little they are trying to cut me off from our world because I know too much about their world.

They have the most amazing way of finding out what I do. You may not even get this letter. I think I shall have to leave this part of the country and go live with my son in San Diego, Cal., if things get any worse, but it is not easy to give up the place you were born in, and where your family has lived for six generations. Also, I would hardly dare sell this house to anybody now that the creatures have taken notice of it. They seem to be trying to get the black stone back and destroy the phonograph record, but I shall not let them if I can help it. My great police dogs always hold them back, for there are very few here as yet, and they are clumsy in getting about. As I have said, their wings are not much use for short flights on earth. I am on the very brink of deciphering that stone—in a very terrible way— and with your knowledge of folklore you may be able to supply the missing links enough to help me. I suppose you know all about the fearful myths antedating the coming of man to the earth—the Yog-Sothoth and Cthulhu cycles—which are hinted at in the *Necronomicon*. I had access to a copy of that once, and hear that you have one in your college library under lock and key.

To conclude, Mr. Wilmarth, I think that with our respective studies we can be very useful to each other. I don't wish to put you in any peril, and suppose I ought to warn you that possession of the stone and the record won't be very safe; but I think you will find any risks worth running for the sake of knowledge. I will drive down to Newfane or Brattleboro to send whatever you authorize me to send, for the express offices there are more to be trusted. I might say that I live quite alone now, since I can't keep hired help any more. They won't stay because of the things that try to get near the house at night, and that keep the dogs barking continually. I am glad I didn't get as deep as this into the business while my wife was alive, for it would have driven her mad.

Hoping that I am not bothering you unduly, and that you will decide to get in touch with me rather than throw this letter into the waste basket as a madman's raving, I am

Yrs. very truly,

HENRY W. AKELEY

P.S. I am making some extra prints of certain photographs taken by me, which I think will help to prove a number of the points I have touched on. The old people think they are monstrously true. I shall send you these very soon if you are interested. H. W. A.

It would be difficult to describe my sentiments upon reading this strange document for the first time. By all ordinary rules, I ought to have laughed more loudly at these extravagances than at the far milder theories which had previously moved me to mirth; yet something in the tone of the letter made me take it with paradoxical seriousness. Not that I believed for a moment in the hidden race from the stars which my correspondent spoke of; but that, after some grave preliminary doubts, I grew to feel oddly sure of his sanity and sincerity, and of his confrontation by some genuine though singular and abnormal phenomenon which he could not explain except in this imaginative way. It could not be as he thought it, I reflected, yet on the other hand, it could not be otherwise than worthy of investigation. The man seemed unduly excited and alarmed about something, but it was hard to think that all cause was lacking. He was so specific and logical in certain ways—and after all, his yarn did fit in so perplexingly well with some of the old myths—even the wildest Indian legends.

That he had really overheard disturbing voices in the hills, and had really found the black stone he spoke about, was wholly possible despite the crazy inferences he had made—inferences probably suggested by the man who had claimed to be a spy of the outer beings and had later killed himself. It was easy to deduce that this man must have been wholly insane, but that he probably had a streak of perverse outward logic which made the naive Akeley—already prepared for such things by his folklore studies—believe his tale. As for the latest developments—it appeared from his inability to keep hired help that Akeley's humbler rustic neighbours were as convinced as he that his house was besieged by uncanny things at night. The dogs really barked, too.

And then the matter of that phonograph record, which I could not but believe he had obtained in the way he said. It must mean something; whether animal noises deceptively like human speech, or the speech of some hidden, night-haunting human being decayed to a state not much above that of lower animals. From this my thoughts went back to the black hieroglyphed stone, and to speculations upon what it might mean. Then, too, what of the photographs which Akeley said he was about to send, and which the old people had found so convincingly terrible?

As I re-read the cramped handwriting I felt as never before that my credulous opponents might have more on their side than I had conceded. After all, there might be some queer and perhaps hereditarily misshapen outcasts in those shunned hills, even though no such race of star-born monsters as folklore claimed. And if there were, then the presence of strange bodies in the flooded streams would not be wholly beyond belief. Was it too presumptuous to suppose that both the old legends and the recent reports had this much of reality behind them? But even as I harboured these doubts I felt ashamed that so fantastic a piece of bizarrerie as Henry Akeley's wild letter had brought them up.

In the end I answered Akeley's letter, adopting a tone of friendly interest and soliciting further particulars. His reply came almost by return mail; and contained, true to promise, a number of kodak views of scenes and objects illustrating what he had to tell. Glancing at these pictures as I took them from the envelope, I felt a curious sense of fright and nearness to forbidden things; for in spite of the vagueness of most of them, they had a damnably suggestive power which was intensified by the fact of their being genuine photographs—actual optical links with what they portrayed, and the product of an impersonal transmitting process without prejudice, fallibility, or mendacity.

The more I looked at them, the more I saw that my serious estimate of Akeley and his story had not been unjustified. Certainly, these pictures carried conclusive evidence of something in the Vermont hills which was at least vastly outside the radius of our common knowledge and belief. The worst thing of all was the footprint—a view taken where the sun shone on a mud patch somewhere in a deserted upland. This was no cheaply counterfeited thing, I could see at a glance; for the sharply defined pebbles and grass-blades in the field of vision gave a clear index of scale and left no possibility of a tricky double exposure. I have called the thing a "footprint," but "claw-print" would be a better term. Even now I can scarcely describe it save to say that it was hideously crab-like, and that there seemed to be some ambiguity about its direction. It was not a very deep or fresh print, but seemed to be about the size of an average man's foot. From a central pad, pairs of saw-toothed nippers projected in opposite directions—quite baffling as to function, if indeed the whole object were exclusively an organ of locomotion.

Another photograph—evidently a time-exposure taken in deep shadow—was of the mouth of a woodland cave, with a boulder of rounded regularity choking the aperture. On the bare ground in front of it one could just discern a dense network of curious tracks, and when I studied the picture with a magnifier I felt uneasily sure that the tracks were like the one in the other view. A third picture shewed a druid-like circle of standing stones on the summit of a wild hill. Around the cryptic circle the grass was very much beaten down and worn away, though I could not detect any footprints even with the glass. The extreme remoteness of the place was apparent from the veritable sea of tenantless mountains which formed the background and stretched away toward a misty horizon.

But if the most disturbing of all the views was that of the footprint, the most curiously suggestive was that of the great black stone found in the Round Hill woods. Akeley had photographed it on what was evidently his study table, for I could see rows of books and a bust of Milton in the background. The thing, as nearly as one might guess, had faced the camera vertically with a somewhat irregularly curved surface of one by two feet; but to say anything definite about that surface, or about the general shape of the whole mass, almost defies the power of language. What outlandish geometrical principles had guided its cutting—for artificially cut it surely was—I could not even begin to guess; and never before had

I seen anything which struck me as so strangely and unmistakably alien to this world. Of the hieroglyphics on the surface I could discern very few, but one or two that I did see gave rather a shock. Of course they might be fraudulent, for others besides myself had read the monstrous and abhorred *Necronomicon* of the mad Arab Abdul Alhazred; but it nevertheless made me shiver to recognise certain ideographs which study had taught me to link with the most blood-curdling and blasphemous whispers of things that had had a kind of mad half-existence before the earth and the other inner worlds of the solar system were made.

Of the five remaining pictures, three were of swamp and hill scenes which seemed to bear traces of hidden and unwholesome tenancy. Another was of a queer mark in the ground very near Akeley's house, which he said he had photographed the morning after a night on which the dogs had barked more violently than usual. It was very blurred, and one could really draw no certain conclusions from it; but it did seem fiendishly like that other mark or claw-print photographed on the deserted upland. The final picture was of the Akeley place itself; a trim white house of two stories and attic, about a century and a quarter old, and with a well-kept lawn and stone-bordered path leading up to a tastefully carved Georgian doorway. There were several huge police dogs on the lawn, squatting near a pleasant-faced man with a close-cropped grey beard whom I took to be Akeley himself—his own photographer, one might infer from the tube-connected bulb in his right hand.

From the pictures I turned to the bulky, closely-written letter itself; and for the next three hours was immersed in a gulf of unutterable horror. Where Akeley had given only outlines before, he now entered into minute details; presenting long transcripts of words overheard in the woods at night, long accounts of monstrous pinkish forms spied in thickets at twilight on the hills, and a terrible cosmic narrative derived from the application of profound and varied scholarship to the endless bygone discourses of the mad self-styled spy who had killed himself. I found myself faced by names and terms that I had heard elsewhere in the most hideous of connections—Yuggoth, Great Cthulhu, Tsathoggua, Yog-Sothoth, R'lyeh, Nyarlathotep, Azathoth, Hastur, Yian, Leng, the Lake of Hali, Bethmoora, the Yellow Sign, L'mur-Kathulos, Bran, and the Magnum Innominandum—and was drawn back through nameless aeons and inconceivable dimensions to worlds of elder, outer entity at which the crazed author of the *Necronomicon* had only guessed in the vaguest way. I was told of the pits of primal life, and of the streams that had trickled down therefrom; and finally, of the tiny rivulets from one of those streams which had become entangled with the destinies of our own earth.

My brain whirled; and where before I had attempted to explain things away, I now began to believe in the most abnormal and incredible wonders. The array of vital evidence was damnably vast and overwhelming; and the cool, scientific attitude of Akeley—an attitude removed as far as imaginable from the demented, the fanatical, the hysterical, or even the extravagantly speculative—had a tremendous effect on my thought and judgment. By the time I laid the frightful letter aside I could understand the fears he had come to entertain, and was ready to do anything in my power to keep people away from those wild, haunted hills. Even now, when time has dulled the impression and made me half question my own experience and horrible doubts, there are things in that letter of Akeley's which I would not quote, or even form into words on paper. I am almost glad that the letter and record and photographs are gone now—and I wish, for reasons I shall soon make clear, that the new planet beyond Neptune had not been discovered.

With the reading of that letter my public debating about the Vermont horror permanently ended. Arguments from opponents remained unanswered or put off with promises, and eventually the controversy petered out into oblivion. During late May and June

I was in constant correspondence with Akeley; though once in a while a letter would be lost, so that we would have to retrace our ground and perform considerable laborious copying. What we were trying to do, as a whole, was to compare notes in matters of obscure mythological scholarship and arrive at a clearer correlation of the Vermont horrors with the general body of primitive world legend.

For one thing, we virtually decided that these morbidities and the hellish Himalayan *Mi-Go* were one and the same order of incarnated nightmare. There was also absorbing zoölogical conjectures, which I would have referred to Professor Dexter in my own college but for Akeley's imperative command to tell no one of the matter before us. If I seem to disobey that command now, it is only because I think that at this stage a warning about those farther Vermont hills—and about those Himalayan peaks which bold explorers are more and more determined to ascend—is more conducive to public safety than silence would be. One specific thing we were leading up to was a deciphering of the hieroglyphics on that infamous black stone—a deciphering which might well place us in possession of secrets deeper and more dizzying than any formerly known to man.

III.

Toward the end of June the phonograph record came—shipped from Brattleboro, since Akeley was unwilling to trust conditions on the branch line north of there. He had begun to feel an increased sense of espionage, aggravated by the loss of some of our letters; and said much about the insidious deeds of certain men whom he considered tools and agents of the hidden beings. Most of all he suspected the surly farmer Walter Brown, who lived alone on a run-down hillside place near the deep woods, and who was often seen loafing around corners in Brattleboro, Bellows Falls,

Newfane, and South Londonderry in the most inexplicable and seemingly unmotivated way. Brown's voice, he felt convinced, was one of those he had overheard on a certain occasion in a very terrible conversation; and he had once found a footprint or claw-print near Brown's house which might possess the most ominous significance. It had been curiously near some of Brown's own footprints—footprints that faced toward it.

So the record was shipped from Brattleboro, whither Akeley drove in his Ford car along the lonely Vermont back roads. He confessed in an accompanying note that he was beginning to be afraid of those roads, and that he would not even go into Townshend for supplies now except in broad daylight. It did not pay, he repeated again and again, to know too much unless one were very remote from those silent and problematical hills. He would be going to California pretty soon to live with his son, though it was hard to leave a place where all one's memories and ancestral feelings centered.

Before trying the record on the commercial machine which I borrowed from the college administration building, I carefully went over all the explanatory matter in Akeley's various letters. This record, he had said, was obtained about 1 a.m. on the first of May, 1915, near the closed mouth of a cave where the wooded west slope of Dark Mountain rises out of Lee's swamp. The place had always been unusually plagued with strange voices, this being the reason he had brought the phonograph, dictaphone, and blank in expectation of results. Former experience had told him that May-Eve—the hideous Sabbat-night of underground European legend—would probably be more fruitful than any other date, and he was not disappointed. It was noteworthy, though, that he never again heard voices at that particular spot.

Unlike most of the overheard forest voices, the substance of the record was quasi-ritualistic, and included one palpably human voice which Akeley had never been able to place. It was not

Brown's, but seemed to be that of a man of greater cultivation. The second voice, however, was the real crux of the thing—for this was the accursed *buzzing* which had no likeness to humanity despite the human words which it uttered in good English grammar and a scholarly accent.

The recording phonograph and dictaphone had not worked uniformly well, and had of course been at a great disadvantage because of the remote and muffled nature of the overheard ritual; so that the actual speech secured was very fragmentary. Akeley had given me a transcript of what he believed the spoken words to be, and I glanced through this again as I prepared the machine for action. The text was darkly mysterious rather than openly horrible, though a knowledge of its origin and manner of gathering gave it all the associative horror which any words could well possess. I will present it here in full as I remember it—and I am fairly confident that I know it correctly by heart, not only from reading the transcript, but from playing the record itself over and over again. It is not a thing which one might readily forget!

(INDISTINGUISHABLE SOUNDS)

(A CULTIVATED MALE HUMAN VOICE)

... is the Lord of the Wood, even to... and the gifts of the men of Leng... so from the wells of night to the gulfs of space, and from the gulfs of space to the wells of night, ever the praises of Great Cthulhu, of Tsathoggua, and of Him Who is not to be Named. Ever Their praises, and abundance to the Black Goat of the Woods. Iä! Shub-Niggurath! The Goat with a Thousand Young!

(A BUZZING IMITATION OF HUMAN SPEECH)

Iä! Shub-Niggurath! The Black Goat of the Woods with a Thousand

Young!

(HUMAN VOICE)

And it has come to pass that the Lord of the Woods, being… seven and nine, down the onyx steps… (tri)butes to Him in the Gulf, Azathoth, He of Whom Thou has taught us marv(els)… on the wings of night out beyond space, out beyond th… to That whereof Yuggoth is the youngest child, rolling alone in black aether at the rim…

(BUZZING VOICE)

… go out among men and find the ways thereof, that He in the Gulf may know. To Nyarlathotep, Mighty Messenger, must all things be told. And He shall put on the semblance of men, the waxen mask and the robe that hides, and come down from the world of Seven Suns to mock…

(HUMAN VOICE)

(Nyarl)athotep, Great Messenger, bringer of strange joy to Yuggoth through the void, Father of the Million Favoured Ones, Stalker among…

(SPEECH CUT OFF BY END OF RECORD)

Such were the words for which I was to listen when I started the phonograph. It was with a trace of genuine dread and reluctance that I pressed the lever and heard the preliminary scratching of the sapphire point, and I was glad that the first faint, fragmentary words were in a human voice—a mellow, educated voice which seemed vaguely Bostonian in accent, and which was certainly not that of any native of the Vermont hills. As I listened to the tantalisingly feeble rendering, I seemed to find the speech identical with Akeley's carefully prepared transcript. On it chanted, in that mellow Bostonian voice... "Iä! Shub-Niggurath! The Goat with a Thousand Young!..."

And then I heard *the other voice*. To this hour I shudder retrospectively when I think of how it struck me, prepared though I was by Akeley's accounts. Those to whom I have since described the record profess to find nothing but cheap imposture or madness in it; but *could they have the accursed thing itself,* or read the bulk of Akeley's correspondence, (especially that terrible and encyclopaedic second letter), I know they would think differently. It is, after all, a tremendous pity that I did not disobey Akeley and play the record for others—a tremendous pity, too, that all of his letters were lost. To me, with my first-hand impression of the actual sounds, and with my knowledge of the background and surrounding circumstances, the voice was a monstrous thing. It swiftly followed the human voice in ritualistic response, but in my imagination it was a morbid echo winging its way across unimaginable abysses from unimaginable outer hells. It is more than two years now since I last ran off that blasphemous waxen cylinder; but at this moment, and at all other moments, I can still hear that feeble, fiendish buzzing as it reached me for the first time.

"Iä! Shub-Niggurath! The Black Goat of the Woods with a Thousand Young!"

But though the voice is always in my ears, I have not even yet been able to analyse it well enough for a graphic description. It was like the drone of some loathsome, gigantic insect ponderously shaped into the articulate speech of an alien species, and I am perfectly certain that the organs producing it can have no resemblance to the vocal organs of man, or indeed to those of any of the mammalia. There were singularities in timbre, range, and overtones which placed this phenomenon wholly outside the sphere of humanity and earth-life. Its sudden advent that first time almost stunned me, and I heard the rest of the record through in a sort of abstracted daze. When the longer passage of buzzing came, there was a sharp intensification of that feeling of blasphemous infinity which had struck me during the shorter and earlier passage. At last the record ended abruptly, during an unusually clear speech of the human and Bostonian voice; but I sat stupidly staring long after the machine had automatically stopped.

I hardly need say that I gave that shocking record many another playing, and that I made exhaustive attempts at analysis and comment in comparing notes with Akeley. It would be both useless and disturbing to repeat here all that we concluded; but I may hint that we agreed in believing we had secured a clue to the source of some of the most repulsive primordial customs in the cryptic elder religions of mankind. It seemed plain to us, also, that there were ancient and elaborate alliances between the hidden outer creatures and certain members of the human race. How extensive these alliances were, and how their state today might compare with their state in earlier ages, we had no means of guessing; yet at best there was room for a limitless amount of horrified speculation. There seemed to be an awful, immemorial linkage in several definite stages betwixt man and nameless infinity. The blasphemies which appeared on earth, it was hinted, came from the dark planet Yuggoth, at the rim of the solar system; but this was itself merely the populous outpost of a frightful interstellar race whose ultimate source must lie far outside even the Einsteinian space-time continuum or greatest known cosmos.

Meanwhile we continued to discuss the black stone and the best way of getting it to Arkham—Akeley deeming it inadvisable to have me visit him at the scene of his nightmare studies. For some reason or other, Akeley was afraid to trust the thing to any ordinary or expected transportation route. His final idea was to take it across country to Bellows Falls and ship it on the Boston and Maine system through Keene and Winchendon and Fitchburg, even though this would necessitate his driving along somewhat lonelier and more forest-traversing hill roads than the main highway to Brattleboro. He said he had noticed a man around the express office at Brattleboro when he had sent the phonograph record, whose actions and expression had been far from reassuring. This man had seemed too anxious to talk with the clerks, and had taken the train on which the record was shipped. Akeley confessed that he had not felt strictly at ease about that record until he heard from me of its safe receipt.

About this time—the second week in July—another letter of mine went astray, as I learned through an anxious communication from Akeley. After that he told me to address him no more at Townshend, but to send all mail in care of the General Delivery at Brattleboro; whither he would make frequent trips either in his car or on the motor-coach line which had lately replaced passenger service on the lagging branch railway. I could see that he was getting more and more anxious, for he went into much detail about the increased barking of the dogs on moonless nights, and about the fresh claw-prints he sometimes found in the road and in the mud at the back of his farmyard when morning came. Once he told about a veritable army of prints drawn up in a line facing an equally thick and resolute line of dog-tracks, and sent a loathsomely disturbing kodak picture to prove it. That was after a night on which the dogs had outdone themselves in barking and howling.

On the morning of Wednesday, July 18, I received a telegram from Bellows Falls, in which Akeley said he was expressing the black stone over the B. & M. on Train No. 5508, leaving Bellows Falls at 12:15 p.m., standard time, and due at the North Station in Boston at 4:12 p.m. It ought, I calculated, to get up to Arkham at least by the next noon; and accordingly I stayed in all Thursday morning to receive it. But noon came and went without its advent, and when I telephoned down to the express office I was informed that no shipment for me had arrived. My next act, performed amidst a growing alarm, was to give a long-distance call to the express agent at the Boston North Station; and I was scarcely surprised to learn that my consignment had not appeared. Train No. 5508 had pulled in only 35 minutes late on the day before, but had contained no box addressed to me. The agent promised, however, to institute a searching inquiry; and I ended the day by sending Akeley a night-letter outlining the situation.

With commendable promptness a report came from the Boston office on the following afternoon, the agent telephoning as soon as he learned the facts. It seemed that the railway express clerk on No. 5508 had been able to recall an incident which might have much bearing on my loss—an argument with a very curious-voiced man, lean, sandy, and rustic-looking, when the train was waiting at Keene, N. H., shortly after one o'clock standard time.

The man, he said, was greatly excited about a heavy box which he claimed to expect, but which was neither on the train nor entered on the company's books. He had given the name of Stanley Adams, and had had such a queerly thick droning voice, that it made the clerk abnormally dizzy and sleepy to listen to him. The clerk could not remember quite how the conversation had ended, but recalled starting into a fuller awakeness when the train began to move. The Boston agent added that this clerk was a young man of wholly unquestioned veracity and reliability, of known antecedents and long with the company.

That evening I went to Boston to interview the clerk in person, having obtained his name and address from the office. He was a frank, prepossessing fellow, but I saw that he could add nothing to his original account. Oddly, he was scarcely sure that he could even recognise the strange inquirer again. Realising that he had no more to tell, I returned to Arkham and sat up till morning writing letters to Akeley, to the express company and to the police department and station agent in Keene. I felt that the strange-voiced man who had so queerly affected the clerk must have a pivotal place in the ominous business, and hoped that Keene station employees and telegraph-office records might tell something about him and about how he happened to make his inquiry when and where he did.

I must admit, however, that all my investigations came to nothing. The queer-voiced man had indeed been noticed around the Keene station in the early afternoon of July 18, and one lounger seemed to couple him vaguely with a heavy box; but he was altogether unknown, and had not been seen before or since. He had not visited the telegraph office or received any message so far as could be learned, nor had any message which might justly be considered a notice of the black stone's presence on No. 5508 come through the office for anyone. Naturally Akeley joined with me in conducting these inquiries, and even made a personal trip to Keene to question the people around the station; but his attitude toward the matter was more fatalistic than mine. He seemed to find the loss of the box a portentous and menacing fulfillment of inevitable tendencies, and had no real hope at all of its recovery. He spoke of the undoubted telepathic and hypnotic powers of the hill creatures and their agents, and in one letter hinted that he did not believe the stone was on this earth any longer. For my part, I was duly enraged, for I had felt there was at least a chance of learning profound and astonishing things from the old, blurred hieroglyphs. The matter would have rankled bitterly in my mind had not Akeley's immediately subsequent letters brought up a new phase of the whole horrible hill problem which at once seized all my attention.

IV.

The unknown things, Akeley wrote in a script grown pitifully tremulous, had begun to close in on him with a wholly new degree of determination. The nocturnal barking of the dogs whenever the moon was dim or absent was hideous now, and there had been attempts to molest him on the lonely roads he had to traverse by day. On the second of August, while bound for the village in his car, he had found a tree-trunk laid in his path at a point where the highway ran through a deep patch of woods; while the savage barking of the two great dogs he had with him told all too well of the things which must have been lurking near. What would have happened had the dogs not been there, he did not dare guess—but he never went out now without at least two of his faithful and powerful pack. Other road experiences had occurred on August fifth and sixth; a shot grazing his car on one occasion, and the barking of the dogs telling of unholy woodland presences on the other.

On August fifteenth I received a frantic letter which disturbed me greatly, and which made me wish Akeley could put aside his lonely reticence and call in the aid of the law. There had been frightful happening on the night of the 12-13th, bullets flying out-side the farmhouse, and three of the twelve great dogs being found shot dead in the morning. There were myriads of claw-prints in the road, with the human prints of Walter Brown among them. Akeley had started to telephone to Brattleboro for more dogs, but the wire had gone dead before he had a chance to say much. Later he went to Brattleboro in his car, and learned there that linemen had found the main cable neatly cut at a point where it ran through the deserted hills north of Newfane. But he was about to start home with four fine new dogs, and several cases of ammuni-tion for his big-game repeating rifle. The letter was written at the post office in Brattleboro, and came through to me without delay.

My attitude toward the matter was by this time quickly slip-ping from a scientific to an alarmedly personal one. I was afraid for Akeley in his remote, lonely farmhouse, and half afraid for myself because of my now definite connection with the strange hill prob-lem. The thing was *reaching out* so. Would it suck me in and engulf me? In replying to his letter I urged him to seek help, and hinted that I might take action myself if he did not. I spoke of visiting Vermont in person in spite of his wishes, and of helping him explain the situation to the proper authorities. In return, however, I received only a telegram from Bellows Falls which read thus:

APPRECIATE YOUR POSITION BUT CAN DO NOTHING TAKE NO ACTION YOURSELF FOR IT COULD ONLY HARM BOTH WAIT FOR EXPLANATION.

HENRY AKELY

But the affair was steadily deepening. Upon my replying to the telegram I received a shaky note from Akeley with the astonishing news that he had not only never sent the wire, but had not received the letter from me to which it was an obvious reply. Hasty inquiries by him at Bellows Falls had brought out that the message was deposited by a strange sandy-haired man with a curiously thick, droning voice, though more than this he could not learn. The clerk showed him the original text as scrawled in pencil by the sender, but the handwriting was wholly unfamiliar. It was noticeable that the signature was misspelled—A-K-E-L-Y, without the second "E." Certain conjectures were inevitable, but amidst the obvious crisis he did not stop to elaborate upon them,

He spoke of the death of more dogs and the purchase of still others, and of the exchange of gunfire which had become a settled feature each moonless night. Brown's prints, and the prints of at least one or two more shod human figures, were now found regularly among the claw-prints in the road, and at the back of the farmyard. It was, Akeley admitted, a pretty bad business; and before long he would probably have to go to live with his California son whether or not he could sell the old place. But it was not easy to leave the only spot one could really think of as home. He must try to hang on a little longer; perhaps he could scare off the intruders—especially if he openly gave up all further attempts to penetrate their secrets.

Writing Akeley at once, I renewed my offers of aid, and spoke again of visiting him and helping him convince the authorities of his dire peril. In his reply he seemed less set against that plan than his past attitude would have led one to predict, but said he would like to hold off a little while longer—long enough to get his things in order and reconcile himself to the idea of leaving an almost morbidly cherished birthplace. People looked askance at his studies and speculations and it would be better to get quietly off without setting the countryside in a turmoil and creating widespread doubts of his own sanity. He had had enough, he admitted, but he wanted to make a dignified exit if he could.

This letter reached me on the twenty-eighth of August, and I prepared and mailed as encouraging a reply as I could. Apparently the encouragement had effect, for Akeley had fewer terrors to report when he acknowledged my note. He was not very optimistic, though, and expressed the belief that it was only the full moon season which was holding the creatures off. He hoped there would not be many densely cloudy nights, and talked vaguely of boarding in Brattleboro when the moon waned. Again I wrote him encouragingly but on September 5th there came a fresh communication which had obviously crossed my letter in the mails; and to this I could not give any such hopeful response. In view of its importance I believe I had better give it in full—as best I can do from memory of the shaky script. It ran substantially as follows:

Monday.

Dear Wilmarth—

A rather discouraging P. S. to my last. Last night was thickly cloudy—though no rain—and not a bit of moonlight got through. Things were pretty bad, and I think the end is getting near, in spite of all we have hoped. After midnight something landed on the roof of the house, and the dogs all rushed up to see what it was. I could hear them snapping and tearing around, and then one managed to get on the roof by jumping from the low ell. There was a terrible fight up there, and I heard a frightful *buzzing* which I'll never forget. And then there was a shocking smell. About the same time bullets came through the window and nearly grazed me. I think the main line of the hill creatures had got close to the house when the dogs divided because of the roof business. What was up there I don't know yet, but I'm afraid the creatures are learning to steer better with their space wings. I put out the light and used the windows for loopholes, and raked all around the house with rifle fire aimed just high enough not to hit the dogs. That seemed to end the business, but in the morning I found great pools of blood in the yard, besides pools of a green sticky stuff that had the worst odour I have ever smelled. I climbed up on the roof and found more of the sticky stuff there. Five of the dogs were killed—I'm afraid I hit one myself by aiming too low, for he was shot in the back. Now I am setting the panes the shots broke, and am going to Brattleboro for more dogs. I guess the men at the kennels think I am crazy. Will drop another note later. Suppose I'll be ready for moving in a week or two, though it nearly kills me to think of it.

Hastily—
AKELEY

But this was not the only letter from Akeley to cross mine. On the next morning—September 6th—still another came; this time a frantic scrawl which utterly unnerved me and put me at a loss what to say or do next. Again I cannot do better than quote the text as faithfully as memory will let me.

Tuesday.

Clouds didn't break, so no moon again—and going into the wane anyhow. I'd have the house wired for electricity and put in a searchlight if I didn't know they'd cut the cables as fast as they could be mended.

I think I am going crazy. It may be that all I have ever written you is a dream or madness. It was bad enough before, but this time it is too much. *They talked to me last night*—talked in that cursed buzzing voice and told me things *that I dare not repeat to you.* I heard them plainly above the barking of the dogs, and once when they were drowned out *a human voice helped them.* Keep out of this, Wilmarth—it is worse than either you or I ever suspected. *They don't mean to let me get to California now—they want to take me off alive, or what theoretically and mentally amounts to alive*—not only to Yuggoth, but beyond that—away outside the galaxy *and possibly beyond the last curved rim of space.* I told them I would-n't go where they wish, *or in the terrible way they propose to take me,* but I'm afraid it will be no use. My place is so far out that they may come by day as well as by night before long. Six more dogs killed, and I felt presences all along the wooded parts of the road when I drove to Brattleboro today.

It was a mistake for me to try to send you that phonograph record and black stone. Better smash the record before it's too late. Will drop you another line tomorrow if I'm still here. Wish I could arrange to get my books and things to Brattleboro and board there. I would run off without anything if I could but something inside my mind holds me back. I can slip out to Brattleboro, where I ought to be safe, but I feel just as much a prisoner there as at the house. And I seem to know that I couldn't get much farther even if I dropped everything and tried. It is horrible—don't get mixed up in this.

Yrs—AKELEY

I did not sleep at all the night after receiving this terrible thing, and was utterly baffled as to Akeley's remaining degree of sanity. The substance of the note was wholly insane, yet the manner of expression—in view of all that had gone before—had a grimly potent quality of convincingness. I made no attempt to answer it, thinking it better to wait until Akeley might have time to reply to my latest communication. Such a reply indeed came on the following day, though the fresh material in it quite overshadowed any of the points brought up by the letter nominally answered. Here is what I recall of the text, scrawled and blotted as it was in the course of a plainly frantic and hurried composition.

Wednesday.

W—

Yr letter came, but it's no use to discuss anything any more. I am fully resigned. Wonder that I have even enough will power left to fight them off. Can't escape even if I were willing to give up everything and run. They'll get me.

Had a letter from them yesterday—R.F.D. man brought it while I was at Brattleboro. Typed and postmarked Bellows Falls. Tells what they want to do with me—I can't repeat it. Look out for yourself, too! Smash that record. Cloudy nights keep up, and moon waning all the time. Wish I dared to get help—it might brace up my will power—but everyone who would dare to come at all would call me crazy unless there happened to be some proof. Couldn't ask people to come for no reason at all—am all out of touch with everybody and have been for years.

But I haven't told you the worst, Wilmarth. Brace up to read this, for it will give you a shock. I am telling the truth, though. It is this—*I have seen and touched one of the things, or part of one of the things.* God, man, but it's awful! It was dead, of course. One of the dogs had it, and I found it near the kennel this morning. I tried to save it in the woodshed to convince people of the whole thing, but it all evaporated in a few hours. Nothing left. You know, all those things in the rivers were seen only on the first morning after the flood. And here's the worst. I tried to photograph it for you, but when I developed the film *there wasn't anything visible except the woodshed.* What can the thing have been made of? I saw it and felt it, and they all leave footprints.

It was surely made of matter—but what kind of matter? The shape can't be described. It was a great crab with a lot of pyramided fleshy rings or knots of thick, ropy stuff covered with feelers where a man's head would be. That green sticky stuff is its blood or juice. And there are more of them due on earth any minute.

Walter Brown is missing—hasn't been seen loafing around any of his usual corners in the villages hereabouts. I must have got him with one of my shots, though the creatures always seem to try to take their dead and wounded away.

Got into town this afternoon without any trouble, but am afraid they're beginning to hold off because they're sure of me. Am writing this in Brattleboro P. O. This may be goodbye—if it is, write my son George Goodenough Akeley, 176 Pleasant St., San Diego, Cal., *but don't come up here.* Write the boy if you don't hear from me in a week, and watch the papers for news.

I'm going to play my last two cards now—if I have the will power left. First to try poison gas on the things (I've got the right chemicals and have fixed up masks for myself and the dogs) and then if that doesn't work, tell the sheriff. They can lock me in a madhouse if they want to—it'll be better than what the other creatures would do. Perhaps I can get them to pay attention to the prints around the house—they are faint, but I can find them every morning. Suppose, though, police would say I faked them somehow; for they all think I'm a queer character.

Must try to have a state policeman spend a night here and see for himself—though it would be just like the creatures to learn about it and hold off that night. They cut my wires whenever I try to telephone in the night—the linemen think it is very queer, and may testify for me if they don't go and imagine I cut them myself. I haven't tried to keep them repaired for over a week now.

I could get some of the ignorant people to testify for me about the reality of the horrors, but everybody laughs at what they say, and anyway, they have shunned my place for so long that they don't know any of the new events. You couldn't get one of those rundown farmers to come within a mile of my house for love or money. The mail-carrier hears what they say and jokes me about it—God! If I only dared tell him how real it is! I think I'll try to get him to notice the prints, but he comes in the afternoon and they're usually about gone by that time. If I kept one by setting a box or pan over it, he'd think surely it was a fake or joke.

Wish I hadn't gotten to be such a hermit, so folks don't drop around as they used to. I've never dared show the black stone or the kodak pictures, or play that record, to anybody but the ignorant people. The others would say I faked the whole business and do nothing but laugh. But I may yet try shewing the pictures. They give those claw-prints clearly, even if the things that made them can't be photographed. What a shame nobody else saw that *thing* this morning before it went to nothing!

But I don't know as I care. After what I've been through, a madhouse is as good a place as any. The doctors can help me make up my mind to get away from this house, and that is all that will save me.

Write my son George if you don't hear soon. Goodbye, smash that record, and don't mix up in this.

Yrs—AKELEY

This letter frankly plunged me into the blackest of terror. I did not know what to say in answer, but scratched off some incoherent words of advice and encouragement and sent them by registered mail. I recall urging Akeley to move to Brattleboro at once, and place himself under the protection of the authorities; adding that I would come to that town with the phonograph record and help convince the courts of his sanity. It was time, too, I think I wrote, to alarm the people generally against this thing in their midst. It will be observed that at this moment of stress my own belief in all Akeley had told and claimed was virtually complete, though I did think his failure to get a picture of the dead monster was due not to any freak of Nature but to some excited slip of his own.

V.

Then, apparently crossing my incoherent note and reaching me Saturday afternoon, September 8th, came that curiously different and calming letter neatly typed on a new machine; that strange letter of reassurance and invitation which must have marked so prodigious a transition in the whole nightmare drama of the lonely hills. Again I will quote from memory—seeking for special reasons to preserve as much of the flavour of the style as I can. It was postmarked Bellows Falls, and the signature as well as the body of the letter was typed—as is frequent with beginners in typing. The text, though, was marvellously accurate for a tyro's work; and I concluded that Akeley must have used a machine at some previous period—perhaps in college. To say that the letter relieved me would be only fair, yet beneath my relief lay a substratum of uneasiness. If Akeley had been sane in his terror, was he now sane in his deliverance? And the sort of "improved rapport" mentioned... what was it? The entire thing implied such a diametrical reversal of Akeley's previous attitude! But here is the substance of the text, carefully transcribed from a memory in which I take some pride.

> Townshend, Vermont,
> Thursday, Sept. 6, 1928.

My dear Wilmarth:—

It gives me great pleasure to be able to set you at rest regarding all the silly things I've been writing you. I say "silly," although by that I mean my frightened attitude rather than my descriptions of certain phenomena. Those phenomena are real and important enough; my mistake had been in establishing an anomalous attitude toward them.

I think I mentioned that my strange visitors were beginning to communicate with me, and to attempt such communication. Last night this exchange of speech became actual. In response to certain signals I admitted to the house a messenger from those outside—a fellow-human, let me hasten to say. He told me much that neither you nor I had even begun to guess, and showed clearly how totally we had misjudged and misinterpreted the purpose of the Outer Ones in maintaining their secret colony on this planet.

It seems that the evil legends about what they have offered to men, and what they wish in connection with the earth, are wholly the result of an ignorant misconception of allegorical speech—speech, of course, moulded by cultural backgrounds and thought-habits vastly different from anything we dream of. My own conjectures, I freely own, shot as widely past the mark as any of the guesses of illiterate farmers and savage Indians. What I had thought morbid and shameful and ignominious is in reality awesome and mind-expanding and even glorious—*my* previous estimate being merely a phase of man's eternal tendency to hate and fear and shrink from the *utterly different*.

Now I regret the harm I have inflicted upon these alien and incredible beings in the course of our nightly skirmishes. If only I had consented to talk peacefully and reasonably with them in the first place! But they bear me no grudge, their emotions being organised very differently from ours. It is their misfortune to have had as their human agents in Vermont some very inferior specimens—the late Walter Brown, for example. He prejudiced me vastly against them. Actually, they have never knowingly harmed men, but have often been cruelly wronged and spied upon by our species. There is a whole secret cult of evil men (a man of your mystical erudition will understand me when I link them with Hastur and the Yellow Sign) devoted to the purpose of tracking them down and injuring them on behalf of monstrous powers from other dimensions. It is against these aggressors—not against normal humanity—that the drastic precautions of the Outer Ones are directed. Incidentally, I learned that many of our lost letters were stolen not by the Outer Ones but by the emissaries of this malign cult.

All that the Outer Ones wish of man is peace and non-molestation and an increasing intellectual rapport. This latter is absolutely necessary now that our inventions and devices are expanding our knowledge and motions, and making it more and more impossible for the Outer Ones' necessary outposts to exist secretly on this planet. The alien beings desire to know mankind more fully, and to have a few of mankind's philosophic and scientific leaders know more about them. With such an exchange of knowledge all perils will pass, and a satisfactory *modus vivendi* be established. The very idea of any attempt to *enslave* or *degrade* mankind is ridiculous.

As a beginning of this improved rapport, the Outer Ones have naturally chosen me—whose knowledge of them is already so considerable—as their primary interpreter on earth. Much was told me last night—facts of the most stupendous and vista-opening nature—and more will be subsequently communicated to me both orally and in writing. I shall not be called upon to make any trip *outside* just yet, though I shall probably *wish* to do so later on—employing special means and transcending everything which we have hitherto been accustomed to regard as human experience. My house will be besieged no longer. Everything has reverted to normal, and the dogs will have no further occupation. In place of terror I have been given a rich boon of knowledge and intellectual adventure which few other mortals have ever shared.

The Outer Beings are perhaps the most marvellous organic things in or beyond all space and time-members of a cosmos-wide race of which all other life-forms are merely degenerate variants. They are more vegetable than animal, if these terms can be applied to the sort of matter composing them, and have a somewhat fungoid structure; though the presence of a chlorophyll-like substance and a very singular nutritive system differentiate them altogether from true cormophytic fungi. Indeed, the type is composed of a form of matter totally alien to our part of space—with electrons having a wholly different vibration-rate. That is why the beings cannot be photographed on the *ordinary* camera films and plates of our known universe, even though our eyes can see them. With proper knowledge, however, any good chemist could make a photographic emulsion which would record their images.

The genus is unique in its ability to traverse the heatless and airless interstellar void in full corporeal form, and some of its variants cannot do this without mechanical aid or curious surgical transpositions. Only a few species have the ether-resisting wings characteristic of the Vermont variety. Those inhabiting certain remote peaks in the Old World were brought in other ways. Their external resemblance to animal life, and to the sort of structure we understand as material, is a matter of parallel evolution rather than of close kinship. Their brain-capacity exceeds that of any other surviving life-form, although the winged types of our hill country are by no means the most highly developed. Telepathy is their usual means of discourse, though they have rudimentary vocal organs which, after a slight operation (for surgery is an incredibly expert and everyday thing among them), can roughly duplicate the speech of such types of organism as still use speech.

Their main *immediate* abode is a still undiscovered and almost lightless planet at the very edge of our solar system—beyond Neptune, and the ninth in distance from the sun. It is, as we have inferred, the object mystically hinted at as "Yuggoth" in certain ancient and forbidden writings; and it will soon be the scene of a strange focussing of thought upon our world in an effort to facilitate mental rapport. I would not be surprised if astronomers become sufficiently sensitive to these thought-currents to discover Yuggoth when the Outer Ones wish them to do so. But Yuggoth, of course, is only the stepping-stone. The main body of the beings inhabits strangely organized abysses wholly beyond the utmost reach of any human imagination. The space-time globule which we recognize as the totality of all cosmic entity is only an atom in the genuine infinity which is theirs. *And as much of this infinity as any human brain can hold is eventually to be opened up to me, as it has been to not more than fifty other men since the human race has existed.*

You will probably call this raving at first, Wilmarth, but in time you will appreciate the titanic opportunity I have stumbled upon. I want you to share as much of it as is possible, and to that end must tell you thousands of things that won't go on paper. In the past I have warned you not to come to see me. Now that all is safe, I take pleasure in rescinding that warning and inviting you.

Can't you make a trip up here before your college term opens? It would be marvelously delightful if you could. Bring along the phonograph record and all my letters to you as consultative data—we shall need them in piecing together the whole tremendous story. You might bring the kodak prints, too, since I seem to have mislaid the negatives and my own prints in all this recent excitement. But what a wealth of facts I have to add to all this groping and tentative material—*and what a stupendous device I have to supplement my additions!*

Don't hesitate—I am free from espionage now, and you will not meet anything unnatural or disturbing. Just come along and let my car meet you at the Brattleboro station—prepare to stay as long as you can, and expect many an evening of discussion of things beyond all human conjecture. Don't tell anyone about it, of course—for this matter must not get to the promiscuous public.

The train service to Brattleboro is not bad—you can get a timetable in Boston. Take the B. & M. to Greenfield, and then change for the brief remainder of the way. I suggest your taking the convenient 4:10 p.m.—standard—from Boston. This gets into Greenfield at 7:35, and at 9:19 a train leaves there which reaches Brattleboro at 10:01. That is week-days. Let me know the date and I'll have my car on hand at the station.

Pardon this typed letter, but my handwriting has grown shaky of late, as you know, and I don't feel equal to long stretches of script. I got this new Corona in Brattleboro yesterday—it seems to work very well.

Awaiting word, and hoping to see you shortly with the phonograph record and all my letters—and the kodak prints—

I am

Yours in anticipation,

HENRY W. AKELEY.

To Albert N. Wilmarth, Esq.,
Miskatonic University,
Arkham, Mass.

The complexity of my emotions upon reading, re-reading, and pondering over this strange and unlooked-for letter is past adequate description. I have said that I was at once relieved and made uneasy, but this expresses only crudely the overtones of diverse and largely subconscious feelings which comprised both the relief and the uneasiness. To begin with, the thing was so antipodally at variance with the whole chain of horrors preceding it—the change of mood from stark terror to cool complacency and even exultation was so unheralded, lightning-like, and complete! I could scarcely believe that a single day could so alter the psychological perspective of one who had written that final frenzied bulletin of Wednesday, no matter what relieving disclosures that day might have brought. At certain moments a sense of conflicting unrealities made me wonder whether this whole distantly reported drama of fantastic forces were not a kind of half-illusory dream created largely within my own mind. Then I thought of the phonograph record and gave way to still greater bewilderment.

The letter seemed so unlike anything which could have been expected! As I analysed my impression, I saw that it consisted of two distinct phases. First, granting that Akeley had been sane before and was still sane, the indicated change in the situation itself was so swift and unthinkable. And secondly, the change in Akeley's own manner, attitude, and language was so vastly beyond the normal or the predictable. The man's whole personality seemed to have undergone an insidious mutation—a mutation so deep that one could scarcely reconcile his two aspects with the supposition that both represented equal sanity. Word-choice, spelling—all were subtly different. And with my academic sensitiveness to prose style, I could trace profound divergences in his commonest reactions and rhythm-responses. Certainly, the emotional cataclysm or revelation which could produce so radical an overturn must be an extreme one indeed! Yet in another way the letter seemed quite characteristic of Akeley. The same old passion for infinity—the same old scholarly inquisitiveness. I could not a moment—or more than a moment—credit the idea of spuriousness or malign substitution. Did not the invitation—the willingness to have me test the truth of the letter in person—prove its genuineness?

I did not retire Saturday night, but sat up thinking of the shadows and marvels behind the letter I had received. My mind, aching from the quick succession of monstrous conceptions it had been forced to confront during the last four months, worked upon this startling new material in a cycle of doubt and acceptance which repeated most of the steps experienced in facing the earlier wonders; till long before dawn a burning interest and curiosity had begun to replace the original storm of perplexity and uneasiness. Mad or sane, metamorphosed or merely relieved, the chances were that Akeley had actually encountered some stupendous change of perspective in his hazardous research; some change at once diminishing his danger—real or fancied—and opening dizzy new vistas of cosmic and superhuman knowledge. My own zeal for the unknown flared up to meet his, and I felt myself touched by the contagion of the morbid barrier-breaking. To shake off the maddening and wearying limitations of time and space and natural law—to be linked with the vast *outside*—to come close to the nighted and abysmal secrets of the infinite and the ultimate—surely such a thing was worth the risk of one's life, soul, and sanity! And Akeley had said there was no longer any peril—he had invited me to visit him instead of warning me away as before. I tingled at the thought of what he might now have to tell me—there was an almost paralysing fascination in the thought of sitting in that lonely and lately-beleaguered farmhouse with a man who had talked with actual emissaries from outer space; sitting there with the terrible record and the pile of letters in which Akeley had summarised his earlier conclusions.

So late Sunday morning I telegraphed Akeley that I would meet him in Brattleboro on the following Wednesday—September 12th—if that date were convenient for him. In only one respect did I depart from his suggestions, and that concerned the choice of a train. Frankly, I did not feel like arriving in that haunted Vermont region late at night; so instead of accepting the train he chose I telephoned the station and devised another arrangement. By rising early and taking the 8:07 a.m. (standard) into Boston, I could catch the 9:25 for Greenfield; arriving there at 12:22 noon. This connected exactly with a train reaching Brattleboro at 1:08 p.m.—a much more comfortable hour than 10:01 for meeting Akeley and riding with him into the close-packed, secret-guarding hills.

I mentioned this choice in my telegram, and was glad to learn in the reply which came toward evening that it had met with my prospective host's endorsement. His wire ran thus:

ARRANGEMENT SATISFACTORY WILL MEET 1:08 TRAIN WEDNESDAY. DON'T FORGET RECORD AND LETTERS AND PRINTS. KEEP DESTINATION QUIET. EXPECT GREAT REVELATIONS.

AKELEY.

Receipt of this message in direct response to one sent to Akeley—and necessarily delivered to his house from the Townshend station either by official messenger or by a restored telephone service—removed any lingering subconscious doubts I may have had about the authorship of the perplexing letter. My relief was marked—indeed, it was greater than I could account for at the time; since all such doubts had been rather deeply buried. But I slept soundly and long that night, and was eagerly busy with preparations during the ensuing two days.

VI.

On Wednesday I started as agreed, taking with me a valise full of simple necessities and scientific data, including the hideous phonograph record, the kodak prints, and the entire file of Akeley's correspondence. As requested, I had told no one where I was going; for I could see that the matter demanded utmost privacy, even allowing for its most favourable turns. The thought of actual mental contact with alien, outside entities was stupefying enough to my trained and somewhat prepared mind; and this being so, what might one think of its effect on the vast masses of uninformed laymen? I do not know whether dread or adventurous expectancy was uppermost in me as I changed trains at Boston and began the long westward run out of familiar regions into those I knew less thoroughly. Waltham—Concord—Ayer—Fitchburg—Gardner—Athol—

My train reached Greenfield seven minutes late, but the north-bound connecting express had been held. Transferring in haste, I felt a curious breathlessness as the cars rumbled on through the early afternoon sunlight into territories I had always read of but had never before visited. I knew I was entering an altogether older-fashioned and more primitive New England than the mechanised, urbanised coastal and southern areas where all my life had been spent; an unspoiled, ancestral New England without the foreigners and factory-smoke, billboards and concrete roads, of the sections which modernity has touched. There would be odd survivals of that continuous native life whose deep roots make it the one authentic outgrowth of the landscape—the continuous native life which keeps alive strange ancient memories, and fertilises the soil for shadowy, marvellous, and seldom-mentioned beliefs.

Now and then I saw the blue Connecticut River gleaming in the sun, and after leaving Northfield we crossed it. Ahead loomed green and cryptical hills, and when the conductor came around I learned that I was at last in Vermont. He told me to set my watch back an hour, since the northern hill country will have no dealings with new-fangled daylight time schemes. As I did so it seemed to me that I was likewise turning the calendar back a century.

The train kept close to the river, and across in New Hampshire I could see the approaching slope of steep Wantastiquet, about which singular old legends cluster. Then streets appeared on my left, and a green island showed in the stream on my right. People rose and filed to the door, and I followed them. The car stopped, and I alighted beneath the long train-shed of the Brattleboro station.

Looking over the line of waiting motors I hesitated a moment to see which one might turn out to be the Akeley Ford, but my identity was divined before I could take the initiative. And yet it was clearly not Akeley himself who advanced to meet me with an outstretched hand and a mellowly phrased query as to whether I was indeed Mr. Albert N. Wilmarth of Arkham. This man bore no resemblance to the bearded, grizzled Akeley of the snapshot; but was a younger and more urbane person, fashionably dressed, and wearing only a small, dark moustache. His cultivated voice held an odd and almost disturbing hint of vague familiarity, though I could not definitely place it in my memory.

As I surveyed him I heard him explaining that he was a friend of my prospective host's who had come down from Townshend in his stead. Akeley, he declared, had suffered a sudden attack of some asthmatic trouble, and did not feel equal to making a trip in the outdoor air. It was not serious, however, and there was to be no change in plans regarding my visit. I could not make out just how much this Mr. Noyes—as he announced himself—knew of Akeley's researches and discoveries, though it seemed to me that his casual manner stamped him as a comparative outsider. Remembering what a hermit Akeley had been, I was a trifle surprised at the ready availability of such a friend; but did not let my puzzlement deter me from entering the motor to which he gestured me. It was not the small ancient car I had expected from Akeley's descriptions, but a large and immaculate specimen of recent pattern—apparently Noyes's own, and bearing Massachusetts license plates with the amusing "sacred codfish" device of that year. My guide, I concluded, must be a summer transient in the Townshend region.

Noyes climbed into the car beside me and started it at once. I was glad that he did not overflow with conversation, for some peculiar atmospheric tensity made me feel disinclined to talk. The town seemed very attractive in the afternoon sunlight as we swept up an incline and turned to the right into the main street. It drowsed like the older New England cities which one remembers from boyhood, and something in the collocation of roofs and steeples and chimneys and brick walls formed contours touching deep viol-strings of ancestral emotion. I could tell that I was at the gateway of a region half-bewitched through the piling-up of unbroken time-accumulations; a region where old, strange things have had a chance to grow and linger because they have never been stirred up.

As we passed out of Brattleboro my sense of constraint and foreboding increased, for a vague quality in the hill-crowded countryside with its towering, threatening, close-pressing green and granite slopes hinted at obscure secrets and immemorial survivals which might or might not be hostile to mankind. For a time our course followed a broad, shallow river which flowed down from unknown hills in the north, and I shivered when my companion told me it was the West River. It was in this stream, I recalled from newspaper items, that one of the morbid crablike beings had been seen floating after the floods.

Gradually the country around us grew wilder and more deserted. Archaic covered bridges lingered fearsomely out of the past in pockets of the hills, and the half-abandoned railway track paralleling the river seemed to exhale a nebulously visible air of desolation. There were awesome sweeps of vivid valley where great cliffs rose, New England's virgin granite showing grey and austere through the verdure that scaled the crests. There were gorges where untamed streams leaped, bearing down toward the river the unimagined secrets of a thousand pathless peaks. Branching away now and then were narrow, half-concealed roads that bored their way through solid, luxuriant masses of forest among whose primal trees whole armies of elemental spirits might well lurk. As I saw these I thought of how Akeley had been molested by unseen agencies on his drives along this very route, and did not wonder that such things could be.

The quaint, sightly village of Newfane, reached in less than an hour, was our last link with that world which man can definitely call his own by virtue of conquest and complete occupancy. After that we cast off all allegiance to immediate, tangible, and time-touched things, and entered a fantastic world of hushed unreality in which the narrow, ribbon-like road rose and fell and curved with an almost sentient and purposeful caprice amidst the tenant-less green peaks and half-deserted valleys. Except for the sound of the motor, and the faint stir of the few lonely farms we passed at infrequent intervals, the only thing that reached my ears was the gurgling, insidious trickle of strange waters from numberless hidden fountains in the shadowy woods.

The nearness and intimacy of the dwarfed, domed hills now became veritably breath-taking. Their steepness and abruptness were even greater than I had imagined from hearsay, and suggested nothing in common with the prosaic objective world we know. The dense, unvisited woods on those inaccessible slopes seemed to harbour alien and incredible things, and I felt that the very outline of the hills themselves held some strange and aeon-forgotten meaning, as if they were vast hieroglyphs left by a rumoured titan race whose glories live only in rare, deep dreams. All the legends of the past, and all the stupefying imputations of Henry Akeley's letters and exhibits, welled up in my memory to heighten the atmosphere of tension and growing menace. The purpose of my visit, and the frightful abnormalities it postulated struck at me all at once with a chill sensation that nearly over-balanced my ardour for strange delvings.

My guide must have noticed my disturbed attitude; for as the road grew wilder and more irregular, and our motion slower and more jolting, his occasional pleasant comments expanded into a steadier flow of discourse. He spoke of the beauty and weirdness of the country, and revealed some acquaintance with the folklore studies of my prospective host. From his polite questions it was obvious that he knew I had come for a scientific purpose, and that I was bringing data of some importance; but he gave no sign of appreciating the depth and awfulness of the knowledge which Akeley had finally reached.

His manner was so cheerful, normal, and urbane that his remarks ought to have calmed and reassured me; but oddly enough, I felt only the more disturbed as we bumped and veered onward into the unknown wilderness of hills and woods. At times it seemed as if he were pumping me to see what I knew of the monstrous secrets of the place, and with every fresh utterance that vague, teasing, baffling *familiarity* in his voice increased. It was not an ordinary or healthy familiarity despite the thoroughly whole-some and cultivated nature of the voice. I somehow linked it with forgotten nightmares, and felt that I might go mad if I recognised it. If any good excuse had existed, I think I would have turned back from my visit. As it was, I could not well do so—and it occurred to me that a cool, scientific conversation with Akeley himself after my arrival would help greatly to pull me together.

Besides, there was a strangely calming element of cosmic beau-ty in the hypnotic landscape through which we climbed and plunged fantastically. Time had lost itself in the labyrinths behind, and around us stretched only the flowering waves of faery and the recaptured loveliness of vanished centuries—the hoary groves, the untainted pastures edged with gay autumnal blossoms, and at vast intervals the small brown farmsteads nestling amidst huge trees beneath vertical precipices of fragrant brier and meadow-grass. Even the sunlight assumed a supernal glamour, as if some special atmosphere or exhalation mantled the whole region. I had seen nothing like it before save in the magic vistas that sometimes form the backgrounds of Italian primitives. Sodoma and Leonardo con-ceived such expanses, but only in the distance, and through the vaultings of Renaissance arcades. We were now burrowing bodily through the midst of the picture, and I seemed to find in its necro-mancy a thing I had innately known or inherited and for which I had always been vainly searching.

Suddenly, after rounding an obtuse angle at the top of a sharp ascent, the car came to a standstill. On my left, across a well-kept lawn which stretched to the road and flaunted a border of white-washed stones, rose a white, two-and-a-half-story house of unusu-al size and elegance for the region, with a congenes of contiguous or arcade-linked barns, sheds, and windmill behind and to the right. I recognised it at once from the snapshot I had received, and was not surprised to see the name of Henry Akeley on the gal-vanised-iron mailbox near the road. For some distance back of the

house a level stretch of marshy and sparsely-wooded land extended, beyond which soared a steep, thickly-forested hillside ending in
a jagged leafy crest. This latter, I knew, was the summit of Dark
Mountain, half way up which we must have climbed already.

Alighting from the car and taking my valise, Noyes asked me
to wait while he went in and notified Akeley of my advent. He
himself, he added, had important business elsewhere, and could
not stop for more than a moment. As he briskly walked up the
path to the house I climbed out of the car myself, wishing to
stretch my legs a little before settling down to a sedentary conversation. My feeling of nervousness and tension had risen to a maximum again now that I was on the actual scene of the morbid
beleaguering described so hauntingly in Akeley's letters, and
I honestly dreaded the coming discussions which were to link me
with such alien and forbidden worlds.

Close contact with the utterly bizarre is often more terrifying
than inspiring, and it did not cheer me to think that this very bit
of dusty road was the place where those monstrous tracks and that
foetid green ichor had been found after moonless nights of fear
and death. Idly I noticed that none of Akeley's dogs seemed to be
about. Had he sold them all as soon as the Outer Ones made peace
with him? Try as I might, I could not have the same confidence in
the depth and sincerity of that peace which appeared in Akeley's
final and queerly different letter. After all, he was a man of much
simplicity and with little worldly experience. Was there not, perhaps, some deep and sinister undercurrent beneath the surface of
the new alliance?

Led by my thoughts, my eyes turned downward to the pow-
dery road surface which had held such hideous testimonies. The
last few days had been dry, and tracks of all sorts cluttered the rut-
ted, irregular highway despite the unfrequented nature of the district. With a vague curiosity I began to trace the outline of some
of the heterogeneous impressions, trying meanwhile to curb the

flights of macabre fancy which the place and its memories suggested. There was something menacing and uncomfortable in the funereal stillness, in the muffled, subtle trickle of distant brooks, and in the crowding green peaks and black-wooded precipices that choked the narrow horizon.

And then an image shot into my consciousness which made those vague menaces and flights of fancy seem mild and insignificant indeed. I have said that I was scanning the miscellaneous prints in the road with a kind of idle curiosity—but all at once that curiosity was shockingly snuffed out by a sudden and paralysing gust of active terror. For though the dust tracks were in general confused and overlapping, and unlikely to arrest any casual gaze, my restless vision had caught certain details near the spot where the path to the house joined the highway; and had recognised beyond doubt or hope the frightful significance of those details. It was not for nothing, alas, that I had pored for hours over the kodak views of the Outer Ones' claw-prints which Akeley had sent. Too well did I know the marks of those loathsome nippers, and that hint of ambiguous direction which stamped the horrors as no creatures of this planet. No chance had been left me for merciful mistake. Here, indeed, in objective form before my own eyes, and surely made not many hours ago, were at least three marks which stood out blasphemously among the surprising plethora of blurred footprints leading to and from the Akeley farmhouse. *They were the hellish tracks of the living fungi from Yuggoth.*

I pulled myself together in time to stifle a scream. After all, what more was there than I might have expected, assuming that I had really believed Akeley's letters? He had spoken of making peace with the things. Why, then, was it strange that some of them had visited his house? But the terror was stronger than the reassurance. Could any man be expected to look unmoved for the first time upon the claw-marks of animate beings from outer depths of space? Just then I saw Noyes emerge from the door and approach with a brisk step. I must, I reflected, keep command of myself, for the chances were that this genial friend knew nothing of Akeley's profoundest and most stupendous probings into the forbidden.

Akeley, Noyes hastened to inform me, was glad and ready to see me; although his sudden attack of asthma would prevent him from being a very competent host for a day or two. These spells hit him hard when they came, and were always accompanied by a debilitating fever and general weakness. He never was good for much while they lasted—had to talk in a whisper, and was very clumsy and feeble in getting about. His feet and ankles swelled, too, so that he had to bandage them like a gouty old beef-eater. Today he was in rather bad shape, so that I would have to attend very largely to my own needs; but he was none the less eager for conversation. I would find him in the study at the left of the front hall—the room where the blinds were shut. He had to keep the sunlight out when he was ill, for his eyes were very sensitive.

As Noyes bade me adieu and rode off northward in his car I began to walk slowly toward the house. The door had been left ajar for me; but before approaching and entering I cast a searching glance around the whole place, trying to decide what had struck me as so intangibly queer about it. The barns and sheds looked trimly prosaic enough, and I noticed Akeley's battered Ford in its capacious, unguarded shelter. Then the secret of the queerness reached me. It was the total silence. Ordinarily a farm is at least moderately murmurous from its various kinds of livestock, but here all signs of life were missing. What of the hens and the dogs? The cows, of which Akeley had said he possessed several, might conceivably be out to pasture, and the dogs might possibly have been sold; but the absence of any trace of cackling or grunting was truly singular.

I did not pause long on the path, but resolutely entered the open house door and closed it behind me. It had cost me a distinct psychological effort to do so, and now that I was shut inside I had a momentary longing for precipitate retreat. Not that the place was in the least sinister in visual suggestion; on the contrary, I thought the graceful late-colonial hallway very tasteful and wholesome, and admired the evident breeding of the man who had furnished it. What made me wish to flee was something very attenuated and indefinable. Perhaps it was a certain odd odour which I thought I noticed—though I well knew how common musty odours are in even the best of ancient farmhouses.

VII.

Refusing to let these cloudy qualms overmaster me, I recalled Noyes's instructions and pushed open the six-panelled, brass-latched white door on my left. The room beyond was darkened as I had known before; and as I entered it I noticed that the queer odour was stronger there. There likewise appeared to be some faint, half-imaginary rhythm or vibration in the air. For a moment the closed blinds allowed me to see very little, but then a kind of apologetic hacking or whispering sound drew my attention to a great easy-chair in the farther, darker corner of the room. Within its shadowy depths I saw the white blur of a man's face and hands; and in a moment I had crossed to greet the figure who had tried to speak. Dim though the light was, I perceived that this was indeed my host. I had studied the kodak picture repeatedly, and there could be no mistake about this firm, weather-beaten face with the cropped, grizzled beard.

But as I looked again my recognition was mixed with sadness and anxiety; for certainly, his face was that of a very sick man. I felt that there must be something more than asthma behind that strained, rigid, immobile expression and unwinking glassy stare; and realised how terribly the strain of his frightful experiences must have told on him. Was it not enough to break any human being—even a younger man than this intrepid delver into the forbidden? The strange and sudden relief, I feared, had come too late to save him from something like a general breakdown. There was a touch of the pitiful in the limp, lifeless way his lean hands rested in his lap. He had on a loose dressing-gown, and was swathed around the head and high around the neck with a vivid yellow scarf or hood.

And then I saw that he was trying to talk in the same hacking whisper with which he had greeted me. It was a hard whisper to catch at first, since the grey moustache concealed all movements of the lips, and something in its timbre disturbed me greatly; but by concentrating my attention I could soon make out its purport surprisingly well. The accent was by no means a rustic one, and the language was even more polished than correspondence had led me to expect.

"Mr. Wilmarth, I presume? You must pardon my not rising. I am quite ill, as Mr. Noyes must have told you; but I could not resist having you come just the same. You know what I wrote in my last letter—there is so much to tell you tomorrow when I shall feel better. I can't say how glad I am to see you in person after all our many letters. You have the file with you, of course? And the kodak prints and records? Noyes put your valise in the hall—I suppose you saw it. For tonight I fear you'll have to wait on yourself to a great extent. Your room is upstairs—the one over this—and you'll see the bathroom door open at the head of the staircase. There's a meal spread for you in the dining-room—right through this door at your right—which you can take whenever you feel like it. I'll be a better host tomorrow—but just now weakness leaves me helpless.

"Make yourself at home—you might take out the letters and pictures and records and put them on the table here before you go upstairs with your bag. It is here that we shall discuss them—you can see my phonograph on that corner stand.

"No, thanks—there's nothing you can do for me. I know these spells of old. Just come back for a little quiet visiting before night, and then go to bed when you please. I'll rest right here—perhaps sleep here all night as I often do. In the morning I'll be far better able to go into the things we must go into. You realise, of course, the utterly stupendous nature of the matter before us. To us, as to only a few men on this earth, there will be opened up gulfs of time and space and knowledge beyond anything within the conception of human science or philosophy.

"Do you know that Einstein is wrong, and that certain objects and forces *can* move with a velocity greater than that of light? With proper aid I expect to go backward and forward in time, and actually *see* and *feel* the earth of remote past and future epochs. You can't imagine the degree to which those beings have carried science. There is nothing they can't do with the mind and body of living organisms. I expect to visit other planets, and even other stars and galaxies. The first trip will be to Yuggoth, the nearest world fully peopled by the beings. It is a strange dark orb at the very rim of our solar system—unknown to earthly astronomers as yet. But I must have written you about this. At the proper time, you know, the beings there will direct thought-currents toward us and cause it to be discovered—or perhaps let one of their human allies give the scientists a hint.

"There are mighty cities on Yuggoth—great tiers of terraced towers built of black stone like the specimen I tried to send you. That came from Yuggoth. The sun shines there no brighter than a star, but the beings need no light. They have other subtler senses, and put no windows in their great houses and temples. Light even hurts and hampers and confuses them, for it does not exist at all in the black cosmos outside time and space where they came from originally. To visit Yuggoth would drive any weak man mad—yet I am going there. The black rivers of pitch that flow under those mysterious Cyclopean bridges—things built by some elder race extinct and forgotten before the beings came to Yuggoth from the ultimate voids—ought to be enough to make any man a Dante or

Poe if he can keep sane long enough to tell what he has seen.

"But remember—that dark world of fungoid gardens and windowless cities isn't really terrible. It is only to us that it would seem so. Probably this world seemed just as terrible to the beings when they first explored it in the primal age. You know they were here long before the fabulous epoch of Cthulhu was over, and remember all about sunken R'lyeh when it was above the waters. They've been inside the earth, too—there are openings which human beings know nothing of—some of them in these very Vermont hills—and great worlds of unknown life down there; blue-litten K'n-yan, red-litten Yoth, and black, lightless N'kai. It's from N'kai that frightful Tsathoggua came—you know, the amorphous, toad-like god-creature mentioned in the Pnakotic Manuscripts and the *Necronomicon* and the Commoriom myth-cycle preserved by the Atlantean high-priest Klarkash-Ton.

"But we will talk of all this later on. It must be four or five o'clock by this time. Better bring the stuff from your bag, take a bite, and then come back for a comfortable chat."

Very slowly I turned and began to obey my host; fetching my valise, extracting and depositing the desired articles, and finally ascending to the room designated as mine. With the memory of that roadside claw-print fresh in my mind, Akeley's whispered paragraphs had affected me queerly; and the hints of familiarity with this unknown world of fungous life—forbidden Yuggoth—made my flesh creep more than I cared to own. I was tremendously sorry about Akeley's illness, but had to confess that his hoarse whisper had a hateful as well as pitiful quality. If only he wouldn't *gloat* so about Yuggoth and its black secrets!

My room proved a very pleasant and well-furnished one, devoid alike of the musty odour and disturbing sense of vibration; and after leaving my valise there I descended again to greet Akeley and take the lunch he had set out for me. The dining-room was just beyond the study, and I saw that a kitchen ell extended still farther in the same direction. On the dining-table an ample array of sandwiches, cake, and cheese awaited me, and a Thermos-bottle beside a cup and saucer testified that hot coffee had not been forgotten. After a well-relished meal I poured myself a liberal cup of coffee, but found that the culinary standard had suffered a lapse in this one detail. My first spoonful revealed a faintly unpleasant acrid taste, so that I did not take more. Throughout the lunch I thought of Akeley sitting silently in the great chair in the darkened next room. Once I went in to beg him to share the repast, but he whispered that he could eat nothing as yet. Later on, just before he slept, he would take some malted milk—all he ought to have that day.

After lunch I insisted on clearing the dishes away and washing them in the kitchen sink—incidentally emptying the coffee which I had not been able to appreciate. Then returning to the darkened study I drew up a chair near my host's corner and prepared for such conversation as he might feel inclined to conduct. The letters, pictures, and record were still on the large centre-table, but for the nonce we did not have to draw upon them. Before long I forgot even the bizarre odour and curious suggestions of vibration.

I have said that there were things in some of Akeley's letters—especially the second and most voluminous one—which I would not dare to quote or even form into words on paper. This hesitancy applies with still greater force to the things I heard whispered that evening in the darkened room among the lonely hills. Of the extent of the cosmic horrors unfolded by that raucous voice I cannot even hint. He had known hideous things before, but what he had learned since making his pact with the Outside Things was almost too much for sanity to bear. Even now I absolutely refused to believe what he implied about the constitution of ultimate infinity, the juxtaposition of dimensions, and the frightful position of our known cosmos of space and time in the unending chain of linked cosmos-atoms which makes up the immediate super-cosmos of curves, angles, and material and semi-material electronic organization.

Never was a sane man more dangerously close to the arcana of basic entity—never was an organic brain nearer to utter annihilation in the chaos that transcends form and force and symmetry. I learned whence Cthulhu first came, and why half the great temporary stars of history had flared forth. I guessed—from hints which made even my informant pause timidly—the secret behind the Magellanic Clouds and globular nebulae, and the black truth veiled by the immemorial allegory of Tao. The nature of the Doels was plainly revealed, and I was told the essence (though not the source) of the Hounds of Tindalos. The legend of Yig, Father of Serpents, remained figurative no longer, and I started with loathing when told of the monstrous nuclear chaos beyond angled space which the *Necronomicon* had mercifully cloaked under the name of Azathoth. It was shocking to have the foulest nightmares of secret myth cleared up in concrete terms whose stark, morbid hatefulness exceeded the boldest hints of ancient and mediaeval mystics. Ineluctably I was led to believe that the first whisperers of these accursed tales must have had discourse with Akeley's Outer Ones, and perhaps have visited outer cosmic realms as Akeley now proposed visiting them.

I was told of the Black Stone and what it implied, and was glad that it had not reached me. My guesses about those hieroglyphics had been all too correct! And yet Akeley now seemed reconciled to the whole fiendish system he had stumbled upon; reconciled and eager to probe farther into the monstrous abyss. I wondered what beings he had talked with since his last letter to me, and whether many of them had been as human as that first emissary he had mentioned. The tension in my head grew insufferable, and I built up all sorts of wild theories about that queer, persistent odour and those insidious hints of vibration in the darkened room.

Night was falling now, and as I recalled what Akeley had written me about those earlier nights I shuddered to think there would be no moon. Nor did I like the way the farmhouse nestled in the lee of that colossal forested slope leading up to Dark Mountain's unvisited crest. With Akeley's permission I lighted a small oil lamp, turned it low, and set it on a distant bookcase beside the ghostly bust of Milton; but afterward I was sorry I had done so, for it made my host's strained, immobile face and listless hands look damnably abnormal and corpse-like. He seemed half-incapable of motion, though I saw him nod stiffly once in a while.

After what he had told, I could scarcely imagine what profounder secrets he was saving for the morrow; but at last it developed that his trip to Yuggoth and beyond—*and my own possible participation in it*—was to be the next day's topic. He must have been amused by the start of horror I gave at hearing a cosmic voyage on my part proposed, for his head wabbled violently when I showed my fear. Subsequently he spoke very gently of how human beings might accomplish—and several times had accomplished—the seemingly impossible flight across the interstellar void. It seemed *that complete human bodies did not indeed make the trip,* but that the prodigious surgical, biological, chemical, and mechanical skill of the Outer Ones had found a way to convey human brains without their concomitant physical structure.

There was a harmless way to extract a brain, and a way to keep the organic residue alive during its absence. The bare, compact cerebral matter was then immersed in an occasionally replenished fluid within an ether-tight cylinder of a metal mined in Yuggoth, certain electrodes reaching through and connecting at will with elaborate instruments capable of duplicating the three vital faculties of sight, hearing, and speech. For the winged fungus-beings to carry the brain-cylinders intact through space was an easy matter. Then, on every planet covered by their civilisation, they would find plenty of adjustable faculty-instruments capable of being connected with the encased brains; so that after a little fitting these travelling intelligences could be given a full sensory and articulate life—albeit a bodiless and mechanical one—at each stage of their journeying through and beyond the space-time continuum. It was as simple as carrying a phonograph record about and playing it wherever a phonograph of corresponding make exists. Of its success there could be no question. Akeley was not afraid. Had it not been brilliantly accomplished again and again?

For the first time one of the inert, wasted hands raised itself and pointed stiffly to a high shelf on the farther side of the room. There, in a neat row, stood more than a dozen cylinders of a metal I had never seen before—cylinders about a foot high and somewhat less in diameter, with three curious sockets set in an isosceles triangle over the front convex surface of each. One of them was linked at two of the sockets to a pair of singular-looking machines that stood in the background. Of their purport I did not need to be told, and I shivered as with ague. Then I saw the hand point to a much nearer corner where some intricate instruments with attached cords and plugs, several of them much like the two devices on the shelf behind the cylinders, were huddled together.

"There are four kinds of instruments here, Wilmarth," whispered the voice. "Four kinds—three faculties each—makes twelve pieces in all. You see there are four different sorts of beings represented in those cylinders up there. Three humans, six fungoid beings who can't navigate space corporeally, two beings from Neptune (God! if you could see the body this type has on its own planet!), and the rest entities from the central caverns of an especially interesting dark star beyond the galaxy. In the principal outpost inside Round Hill you'll now and then find more cylinders and machines—cylinders of extra-cosmic brains with different senses from any we know—allies and explorers from the uttermost Outside—and special machines for giving them impressions and expression in the several ways suited at once to them and to the comprehensions of different types of listeners. Round Hill, like most of the beings' main outposts all through the various universes, is a very cosmopolitan place. Of course, only the more common types have been lent to me for experiment.

"Here—take the three machines I point to and set them on the table. That tall one with the two glass lenses in front—then the box with the vacuum tubes and sounding-board—and now the one with the metal disc on top. Now for the cylinder with the label 'B-67' pasted on it. Just stand in that Windsor chair to reach the shelf. Heavy? Never mind! Be sure of the number—B-67. Don't bother that fresh, shiny cylinder joined to the two testing instruments—the one with my name on it. Set B-67 on the table near where you've put the machines—and see that the dial switch on all three machines is jammed over to the extreme left.

"Now connect the cord of the lens machine with the upper socket on the cylinder—there! Join the tube machine to the lower left-hand socket, and the disc apparatus to the outer socket. Now move all the dial switches on the machine over to the extreme right—first the lens one, then the disc one, and then the tube one. That's right. I might as well tell you that this is a human being—just like any of us. I'll give you a taste of some of the others tomorrow."

To this day I do not know why I obeyed those whispers so slavishly, or whether I thought Akeley was mad or sane. After what had gone before, I ought to have been prepared for anything; but this mechanical mummery seemed so like the typical vagaries of crazed inventors and scientists that it struck a chord of doubt which even the preceding discourse had not excited. What the whisperer implied was beyond all human belief—yet were not the other things still farther beyond, and less preposterous only because of their remoteness from tangible concrete proof?

As my mind reeled amidst this chaos, I became conscious of a mixed grating and whirring from all three of the machines lately linked to the cylinder—a grating and whirring which soon subsided into a virtual noiselessness. What was about to happen? Was I to hear a voice? And if so, what proof would I have that it was not some cleverly concocted radio device talked into by a concealed but closely watched speaker? Even now I am unwilling to swear just what I heard, or just what phenomenon really took place before me. But something certainly seemed to take place.

To be brief and plain, the machine with the tubes and sound-box began to speak, and with a point and intelligence which left no doubt that the speaker was actually present and observing us. The voice was loud, metallic, lifeless, and plainly mechanical in every detail of its production. It was incapable of inflection or expressiveness, but scraped and rattled on with a deadly precision and deliberation.

"Mr. Wilmarth," it said, "I hope I do not startle you. I am a human being like yourself, though my body is now resting safely under proper vitalising treatment inside Round Hill, about a mile and a half east of here. I myself am here with you—my brain is in that cylinder and I see, hear, and speak through these electronic vibrators. In a week I am going across the void as I have been many times before, and I expect to have the pleasure of Mr. Akeley's company. I wish I might have yours as well; for I know you by sight and reputation, and have kept close track of your correspondence with our friend. I am, of course, one of the men who have become allied with the outside beings visiting our planet. I met them first in the Himalayas, and have helped them in various ways. In return they have given me experiences such as few men have ever had.

"Do you realise what it means when I say I have been on thirty-seven different celestial bodies—planets, dark stars, and less definable objects—including eight outside our galaxy and two outside the curved cosmos of space and time? All this has not harmed me in the least. My brain has been removed from my body by fissions so adroit that it would be crude to call the operation surgery. The visiting beings have methods which make these extractions easy and almost normal—and one's body never ages when the brain is out of it. The brain, I may add, is virtually immortal with its mechanical faculties and a limited nourishment supplied by occasional changes of the preserving fluid.

"Altogether, I hope most heartily that you will decide to come with Mr. Akeley and me. The visitors are eager to know men of knowledge like yourself, and to show them the great abysses that most of us have had to dream about in fanciful ignorance. It may seem strange at first to meet them, but I know you will be above minding that. I think Mr. Noyes will go along, too—the man who doubtless brought you up here in his car. He has been one of us for years—I suppose you recognised his voice as one of those on the record Mr. Akeley sent you."

At my violent start the speaker paused a moment before concluding.

"So Mr. Wilmarth, I will leave the matter to you; merely adding that a man with your love of strangeness and folklore ought never to miss such a chance as this. There is nothing to fear. All transitions are painless; and there is much to enjoy in a wholly mechanised state of sensation. When the electrodes are disconnected, one merely drops off into a sleep of especially vivid and fantastic dreams.

"And now, if you don't mind, we might adjourn our session till tomorrow. Good night—just turn all the switches back to the left; never mind the exact order, though you might let the lens machine be last. Good night, Mr. Akeley—treat our guest well! Ready now with those switches?"

That was all. I obeyed mechanically and shut off all three switches, though dazed with doubt of everything that had occurred. My head was still reeling as I heard Akeley's whispering voice telling me that I might leave all the apparatus on the table just as it was. He did not essay any comment on what had happened, and indeed no comment could have conveyed much to my burdened faculties. I heard him telling me I could take the lamp to use in my room, and deduced that he wished to rest alone in the dark. It was surely time he rested, for his discourse of the afternoon and evening had been such as to exhaust even a vigorous man. Still dazed, I bade my host good night and went upstairs with the lamp, although I had an excellent pocket flashlight with me.

I was glad to be out of that downstairs study with the queer odour and vague suggestions of vibration, yet could not of course escape a hideous sense of dread and peril and cosmic abnormality as I thought of the place I was in and the forces I was meeting. The wild, lonely region, the black, mysteriously forested slope towering so close behind the house; the footprint in the road, the sick, motionless whisperer in the dark, the hellish cylinders and machines, and above all the invitations to strange surgery and stranger voyagings—these things, all so new and in such sudden succession, rushed in on me with a cumulative force which sapped my will and almost undermined my physical strength.

To discover that my guide Noyes was the human celebrant in that monstrous bygone Sabbat-ritual on the phonograph record was a particular shock, though I had previously sensed a dim, repellent familiarity in his voice. Another special shock came from my own attitude toward my host whenever I paused to analyse it; for much as I had instinctively liked Akeley as revealed in his correspondence, I now found that he filled me with a distinct repulsion. His illness ought to have excited my pity; but instead, it gave me a kind of shudder. He was so rigid and inert and corpselike— and that incessant whispering was so hateful and unhuman!

It occurred to me that this whispering was different from anything else of the kind I had ever heard; that, despite the curious motionlessness of the speaker's moustache-screened lips, it had a latent strength and carrying-power remarkable for the wheezing of an asthmatic. I had been able to understand the speaker when wholly across the room, and once or twice it had seemed to me that the faint but penetrant sounds represented not so much weakness as deliberate repression—for what reason I could not guess.

From the first I had felt a disturbing quality in their timbre. Now, when I tried to weigh the matter, I thought I could trace this impression to a kind of subconscious familiarity like that which had made Noyes's voice so hazily ominous. But when or where I had encountered the thing it hinted at, was more than I could tell.

One thing was certain—I would not spend another night here. My scientific zeal had vanished amidst fear and loathing, and I felt nothing now but a wish to escape from this net of morbidity and unnatural revelation. I knew enough now. It must indeed be true that strange cosmic linkages do exist—but such things are surely not meant for normal human beings to meddle with.

Blasphemous influences seemed to surround me and press chokingly upon my senses. Sleep, I decided, would be out of the question; so I merely extinguished the lamp and threw myself on the bed fully dressed. No doubt it was absurd, but I kept ready for some unknown emergency; gripping in my right hand the revolver I had brought along, and holding the pocket flashlight in my left. Not a sound came from below, and I could imagine how my host was sitting there with cadaverous stiffness in the dark.

Somewhere I heard a clock ticking, and was vaguely grateful for the normality of the sound. It reminded me, though, of another thing about the region which disturbed me—the total absence of animal life. There were certainly no farm beasts about, and now I realised that even the accustomed night-noises of wild living things were absent. Except for the sinister trickle of distant unseen waters, that stillness was anomalous—interplanetary—and I wondered what star-spawned, intangible blight could be hanging over the region. I recalled from old legends that dogs and other beasts had always hated the Outer Ones, and thought of what those tracks in the road might mean.

VIII.

Do not ask me how long my unexpected lapse into slumber lasted, or how much of what ensued was sheer dream. If I tell you that I awakened at a certain time, and heard and saw certain things, you will merely answer that I did not wake then; and that everything was a dream until the moment when I rushed out of the house, stumbled to the shed where I had seen the old Ford, and seized that ancient vehicle for a mad, aimless race over the haunted hills which at last landed me—after hours of jolting and winding through forest-threatened labyrinths—in a village which turned out to be Townshend.

You will also, of course, discount everything else in my report; and declare that all the pictures, record-sounds, cylinder-and-machine sounds, and kindred evidences were bits of pure deception practiced on me by the missing Henry Akeley. You will even hint that he conspired with other eccentrics to carry out a silly and elaborate hoax—that he had the express shipment removed at Keene, and that he had Noyes make that terrifying wax record. It is odd, though, that Noyes has not ever yet been identified; that he was unknown at any of the villages near Akeley's place, though he must have been frequently in the region. I wish I had stopped to memorize the license-number of his car—or perhaps it is better after all that I did not. For I, despite all you can say, and despite all I sometimes try to say to myself, know that loathsome outside influences must be lurking there in the half-unknown hills—and that those influences have spies and emissaries in the world of men. To keep as far as possible from such influences and such emissaries is all that I ask of life in future.

When my frantic story sent a sheriff's posse out to the farmhouse, Akeley was gone without leaving a trace. His loose dressing gown, yellow scarf, and foot-bandages lay on the study floor near his corner easy-chair, and it could not be decided whether any of his other apparel had vanished with him. The dogs and livestock were indeed missing, and there were some curious bullet-holes both on the house's exterior and on some of the walls within; but beyond this nothing unusual could be detected. No cylinders or machines, none of the evidences I had brought in my valise, no queer odour or vibration-sense, no footprints in the road, and none of the problematical things I glimpsed at the very last.

I stayed a week in Brattleboro after my escape, making inquiries among people of every kind who had known Akeley; and the results convince me that the matter is no figment of dream or delusion. Akeley's queer purchase of dogs and ammunition and chemicals, and the cutting of his telephone wires, are matters of record; while all who knew him—including his son in California—concede that his occasional remarks on strange studies had a certain consistency. Solid citizens believe he was mad, and unhesitatingly pronounce all reported evidences mere hoaxes devised with insane cunning and perhaps abetted by eccentric associates; but the lowlier country folk sustain his statements in every detail. He had showed some of these rustics his photographs and black stone, and had played the hideous record for them; and they all said the footprints and buzzing voice were like those described in ancestral legends.

They said, too, that suspicious sights and sounds had been noticed increasingly around Akeley's house after he found the black stone, and that the place was now avoided by everybody except the mail man and other casual, tough-minded people. Dark Mountain and Round Hill were both notoriously haunted spots, and I could find no one who had ever closely explored either. Occasional disappearances of natives throughout the district's history were well attested, and these now included the semi-vagabond Walter Brown, whom Akeley's letters had mentioned. I even came upon one farmer who thought he had personally glimpsed one of the queer bodies at flood-time in the swollen

West River, but his tale was too confused to be really valuable.

When I left Brattleboro I resolved never to go back to Vermont, and I feel quite certain I shall keep my resolution. Those wild hills are surely the outpost of a frightful cosmic race—as I doubt all the less since reading that a new ninth planet has been glimpsed beyond Neptune, just as those influences had said it would be glimpsed. Astronomers, with a hideous appropriateness they little suspect, have named this thing "Pluto." I feel, beyond question, that it is nothing less than nighted Yuggoth—and I shiver when I try to figure out the real reason *why* its monstrous denizens wish it to be known in this way at this especial time. I vainly try to assure myself that these daemoniac creatures are not gradually leading up to some new policy hurtful to the earth and its normal inhabitants.

But I have still to tell of the ending of that terrible night in the farmhouse. As I have said, I did finally drop into a troubled doze; a doze filled with bits of dream which involved monstrous landscape-glimpses. Just what awaked me I cannot yet say, but that I did indeed awake at this given point I feel very certain. My first confused impression was of stealthily creaking floor-boards in the hall outside my door, and of a clumsy, muffled fumbling at the latch. This, however, ceased almost at once; so that my really clear impressions begin with the voices heard from the study below. There seemed to be several speakers, and I judged that they were controversially engaged.

By the time I had listened a few seconds I was broad awake, for the nature of the voices was such as to make all thought of sleep ridiculous. The tones were curiously varied, and no one who had listened to that accursed phonograph record could harbour any doubts about the nature of at least two of them. Hideous though the idea was, I knew that I was under the same roof with nameless things from abysmal space; for those two voices were unmistakably the blasphemous buzzings which the Outside Beings used in their communication with men. The two were individually different—different in pitch, accent, and tempo—but they were both of the same damnable general kind.

A third voice was indubitably that of a mechanical utterance-machine connected with one of the detached brains in the cylinders. There was as little doubt about that as about the buzzings; for the loud, metallic, lifeless voice of the previous evening, with its inflectionless, expressionless scraping and rattling, and its impersonal precision and deliberation, had been utterly unforgettable. For a time I did not pause to question whether the intelligence behind the scraping was the identical one which had formerly talked to me; but shortly afterward I reflected that *any* brain would emit vocal sounds of the same quality if linked to the same mechanical speech-producer; the only possible differences being in language, rhythm, speed, and pronunciation. To complete the eldritch colloquy there were two actually human voices—one the crude speech of an unknown and evidently rustic man, and the other the suave Bostonian tones of my erstwhile guide Noyes.

As I tried to catch the words which the stoutly-fashioned floor so bafflingly intercepted, I was also conscious of a great deal of stirring and scratching and shuffling in the room below; so that I could not escape the impression that it was full of living beings—many more than the few whose speech I could single out. The exact nature of this stirring is extremely hard to describe, for very few good bases of comparison exist. Objects seemed now and then to move across the room like conscious entities; the sound of their footfalls having something about it like a loose, hard-surfaced clattering—as of the contact of ill-coordinated surfaces of horn or hard rubber. It was, to use a more concrete but less accurate comparison, as if people with loose, splintery wooden shoes were shambling and rattling about on the polished board floor. Of the nature and appearance of those responsible for the sounds, I did not care to speculate.

Before long I saw that it would be impossible to distinguish any connected discourse. Isolated words—including the names of Akeley and myself—now and then floated up, especially when uttered by the mechanical speech-producer; but their true significance was lost for want of continuous context. Today I refuse to form any definite deductions from them, and even their frightful effect on me was one of *suggestion* rather than of *revelation*. A terrible and abnormal conclave, I felt certain, was assembled below me; but for what shocking deliberations I could not tell. It was curious how this unquestioned sense of the malign and the blasphemous pervaded me despite Akeley's assurances of the Outsider's friendliness.

With patient listening I began to distinguish clearly between voices, even though I could not grasp much of what any of the voices said. I seemed to catch certain typical emotions behind some of the speakers. One of the buzzing voices, for example, held an unmistakable note of authority; whilst the mechanical voice, notwithstanding its artificial loudness and regularity, seemed to be in a position of subordination and pleading. Noyes's tones exuded a kind of conciliatory atmosphere. The others I could make no attempt to interpret. I did not hear the familiar whisper of Akeley, but well knew that such a sound could never penetrate the solid flooring of my room.

I will try to set down some of the few disjointed words and other sounds I caught, labelling the speakers of the words as best I know how. It was from the speech-machine that I first picked up a few recognisable phrases.

(THE SPEECH-MACHINE)

"... brought it on myself... sent back the letters and the record... end on it... taken in... seeing and hearing... damn you... impersonal force, after all... fresh, shiny cylinder... great God...."

(FIRST BUZZING VOICE)

"... time we stopped... small and human... Akeley... brain... saying...."

(SECOND BUZZING VOICE)

"Nyarlathotep... Wilmarth... records and letters... cheap imposture...."

(NOYES)

"... (an unpronounceable word or name, possibly *N'gah-Kthun*) harmless... peace... couple of weeks... theatrical... told you that before...."

(FIRST BUZZING VOICE)

"... no reason... original plan... effects... Noyes can watch Round Hill... fresh cylinder... Noyes's car...."

(NOYES)

"... well... all yours... down here... rest... place...."

(SEVERAL VOICES AT ONCE IN
INDISTINGUISHABLE SPEECH)

(MANY FOOTSTEPS, INCLUDING THE PECULIAR
LOOSE STIRRING OR CLATTERING)

(A CURIOUS SORT OF FLAPPING SOUND)

(THE SOUND OF AN AUTOMOBILE
STARTING AND RECEDING)

(SILENCE)

That is the substance of what my ears brought me as I lay rigid upon that strange upstairs bed in the haunted farmhouse among the daemoniac hills—lay there fully dressed, with a revolver clenched in my right hand and a pocket flashlight gripped in my left. I became, as I have said, broad awake; but a kind of obscure paralysis nevertheless kept me inert till long after the last echoes of the sounds had died away. I heard the wooden, deliberate ticking of the ancient Connecticut clock somewhere far below, and at last made out the irregular snoring of a sleeper. Akeley must have dozed off after the strange session, and I could well believe that he needed to do so.

Just what to think or what to do was more than I could decide After all, what *had* I heard beyond things which previous information might have led me to expect? Had I not known that the nameless Outsiders were now freely admitted to the farmhouse? No doubt Akeley had been surprised by an unexpected visit from them. Yet something in that fragmentary discourse had chilled me immeasurably, raised the most grotesque and horrible doubts, and made me wish fervently that I might wake up and prove everything a dream. I think my subconscious mind must have caught something which my consciousness has not yet recognised. But what of Akeley? Was he not my friend, and would he not have protested if any harm were meant me? The peaceful snoring below seemed to cast ridicule on all my suddenly intensified fears.

Was it possible that Akeley had been imposed upon and used as a lure to draw me into the hills with the letters and pictures and phonograph record? Did those beings mean to engulf us both in a common destruction because we had come to know too much? Again I thought of the abruptness and unnaturalness of that change in the situation which must have occurred between Akeley's penultimate and final letters. Something, my instinct told me, was terribly wrong. All was not as it seemed. That acrid coffee which I refused—had there not been an attempt by some hidden, unknown entity to drug it? I must talk to Akeley at once, and restore his sense of proportion. They had hypnotised him with their promises of cosmic revelations, but now he must listen to reason. We must get out of this before it would be too late. If he lacked the will power to make the break for liberty. I would supply it. Or if I could not persuade him to go, I could at least go myself. Surely he would let me take his Ford and leave it in a garage in Brattleboro. I had noticed it in the shed—the door being left unlocked and open now that peril was deemed past—and I believed there was a good chance of its being ready for instant use. That momentary dislike of Akeley which I had felt during and after the evening's conversation was all gone now. He was in a position much like my own, and we must stick together. Knowing his indisposed condition, I hated to wake him at this juncture, but I knew that I must. I could not stay in this place till morning as matters stood.

At last I felt able to act, and stretched myself vigorously to regain command of my muscles. Arising with a caution more impulsive than deliberate, I found and donned my hat, took my valise, and started downstairs with the flashlight's aid. In my nervousness I kept the revolver clutched in my right hand, being able to take care of both valise and flashlight with my left. Why I exerted these precautions I do not really know, since I was even then on my way to awaken the only other occupant of the house.

As I half-tiptoed down the creaking stairs to the lower hall I could hear the sleeper more plainly, and noticed that he must be in the room on my left—the living-room I had not entered. On my right was the gaping blackness of the study in which I had heard the voices. Pushing open the unlatched door of the living-room I traced a path with the flashlight toward the source of the snoring, and finally turned the beams on the sleeper's face. But in the next second I hastily turned them away and commenced a cat-like retreat to the hall, my caution this time springing from reason as well as from instinct. For the sleeper on the couch was not Akeley at all, but my quondam guide Noyes.

Just what the real situation was, I could not guess; but common sense told me that the safest thing was to find out as much as possible before arousing anybody. Regaining the hall, I silently closed and latched the living-room door after me; thereby lessening the chances of awakening Noyes. I now cautiously entered the dark study, where I expected to find Akeley, whether asleep or awake, in the great corner chair which was evidently his favorite resting-place. As I advanced, the beams of my flashlight caught the great centre-table, revealing one of the hellish cylinders with sight and hearing machines attached, and with a speech machine standing close by, ready to be connected at any moment. This, I reflected, must be the encased brain I had heard talking during the frightful conference; and for a second I had a perverse impulse to attach the speech machine and see what it would say.

It must, I thought, be conscious of my presence even now; since the sight and hearing attachments could not fail to disclose the rays of my flashlight and the faint creaking of the floor beneath my feet. But in the end I did not dare meddle with the thing. I idly saw that it was the fresh shiny cylinder with Akeley's name on it, which I had noticed on the shelf earlier in the evening and which my host had told me not to bother. Looking back at that moment, I can only regret my timidity and wish that I had boldly caused the apparatus to speak. God knows what mysteries and horrible doubts and questions of identity it might have cleared up! But then, it may be merciful that I let it alone.

From the table I turned my flashlight to the corner where I thought Akeley was, but found to my perplexity that the great easy-chair was empty of any human occupant asleep or awake. From the seat to the floor there trailed voluminously the familiar old dressing-gown, and near it on the floor lay the yellow scarf and the huge foot-bandages I had thought so odd. As I hesitated, striving to conjecture where Akeley might be, and why he had so suddenly discarded his necessary sick-room garments, I observed that the queer odour and sense of vibration were no longer in the room. What had been their cause? Curiously it occurred to me that I had noticed them only in Akeley's vicinity. They had been strongest where he sat, and wholly absent except in the room with him or just outside the doors of that room. I paused, letting the flashlight wander about the dark study and racking my brain for explanations of the turn affairs had taken.

Would to Heaven I had quietly left the place before allowing that light to rest again on the vacant chair. As it turned out, I did not leave quietly; but with a muffled shriek which must have disturbed, though it did not quite awake, the sleeping sentinel across the hall. That shriek, and Noyes's still-unbroken snore, are the last sounds I ever heard in that morbidity-choked farmhouse beneath the black-wooded crest of haunted mountain—that focus of transcosmic horror amidst the lonely green hills and curse-muttering brooks of a spectral rustic land.

It is a wonder that I did not drop flashlight, valise, and revolver in my wild scramble, but somehow I failed to lose any of these. I actually managed to get out of that room and that house without making any further noise, to drag myself and my belongings safely into the old Ford in the shed, and to set that archaic vehicle in motion toward some unknown point of safety in the black, moonless night. The ride that followed was a piece of delirium out of Poe or Rimbaud or the drawings of Doré, but finally I reached Townshend. That is all. If my sanity is still unshaken, I am lucky. Sometimes I fear what the years will bring, especially since that new planet Pluto has been so curiously discovered.

As I have implied, I let my flashlight return to the vacant easy-chair after its circuit of the room; then noticing for the first time the presence of certain objects in the seat, made inconspicuous by the adjacent loose folds of the empty dressing-gown. These are the objects, three in number, which the investigators did not find when they came later on. As I said at the outset, there was nothing of actual visual horror about them. The trouble was in what they led one to infer. Even now I have my moments of half-doubt—moments in which I half-accept the scepticism of those who attribute my whole experience to dream and nerves and delusion.

The three things were damnably clever constructions of their kind, and were furnished with ingenious metallic clamps to attach them to organic developments of which I dare not form any conjecture. I hope—devoutly hope—that they were the waxen products of a master artist, despite what my inmost fears tell me. Great God! That whisperer in darkness with its morbid odour and vibrations! Sorcerer, emissary, changeling, outsider... that hideous repressed buzzing... and all the time in that fresh, shiny cylinder on the shelf... poor devil... "Prodigious surgical, biological, chemical, and mechanical skill"...

For the things in the chair, perfect to the last, subtle detail of microscopic resemblance—or identity—were the face and hands of Henry Wentworth Akeley.

BRIEF BIBLIOGRAPHY
LOVECRAFT LITERATURE AVAILABLE IN FRENCH
by MICHEL HOUELLEBECQ

I. LOVECRAFT'S WORKS

Dans l'abîme du temps and *La couleur tombée du ciel* (Denoël, «Présence du Futur», or J'ai lu)
> The "great texts."

Dagon (J'ai lu or Belfond).
> Some stories are as good as the "great texts," others frankly don't work at all. A prodigious variety of settings and *époques*. An eclectic, bizarre, and in the end very successful collection.

Fungi de Yuggoth et autres poèmes fantastiques (Néo, out of print).
> Lovecraft's poems are surprisingly beautiful, but all their musicality disappears in translation. Fortunately, this is a bilingual edition.

Par-delà le mur du sommeil and *Je suis d'ailleurs* (Denoël, «Présence du Futur» or J'ai lu).
> A selection of fine stories.

II. BOOKS ABOUT H. P. LOVECRAFT

1. *Le Necronomicon,* a collective work (J'ai lu or Belfond).
   This small book aims to sow trouble in the mind... and succeeds. Was HPL *really* among the initiated? A work apart, really.

2. *H.P. Lovecraft, Lettres 1* (Christian Bourgois).
   A selection of letters from the first part of Lovecraft's life (up
   till 1926). Interesting and moving. With a fine preface by
   Francis Lacassin.

3. *H.P. Lovecraft, le roman d'une vie,* Lyon Sprague de Camp (Néo,
   out of print).
   The author lacks true affection for Lovecraft but does his work
   very well. All the qualities of American biography.

TRANSLATOR'S NOTES

Michel Houellebecq cites several French editions of Lovecraft's stories and letters. These citations are interspersed throughout the text. Some are long, while others consist of only two or three words in quotation marks in the middle of one of Houellebecq's sentences. No references indicate the exact source of each citation.

Wishing to use Lovecraft's original English for these quotations, I looked for them in the available editions of Lovecraft's correspondence and stories. I also consulted S. T. Joshi, the renowned Lovecraft scholar. He in turn referred some of my questions to David Schultz, another Lovecraft specialist. Although they helped me find several additional citations, in the final translation several instances remain where it wasn't possible to identify the original English source. Houellebecq was also unable to assist in locating or identifying these citations. In most instances I have resorted to dropping the quotation marks from the original citation and settling for a translation of the French words into English. The following notes indicate where these instances occur.

Houellebecq's French sources, included in the French edition of this book, begin on page 239. The sources that were used to identify the citations in English are on page 245.

page 45:

> a seeker, one who "thirsts for knowledge"

I am unable to find Lovecraft's original phrase corresponding with Houellebecq's *"avide de savoir."*

page 47:

> must not overuse adjectives such as monstrous, unnameable, and unmentionable.

I am unable to find Lovecraft's original phrase corresponding with Houellebecq's *"ne pas abuser des adjectives tel que monstrueux, innommable, indicible…"*

page 48:

> the small thirty-page manuscript entitled *The Commonplace Book.*

Houellebecq is referring to *Le Livre de Raison,* a translation of the *Commonplace Book,* along with "Notes on Weird Fiction" (1933), "Weird Story Plots" (1933), and "Notes on Writing Weird Fiction" (1934) that appear in *Lovecraft* (Paris: Robert Laffont, 1991), Vol. 1, pp. 1051-73. *"Livre de raison"* is commonly translated as "ledger."

page 58:

> *"In a word, Child, I look upon this sort of writing as a mere prying survey of the lowest part of life, and a slavish transcript of simple events made with the crude feelings of a porter or bargeman [and without any native genius or colour of the creative imagination whatever...]"*

Houellebecq omits a segment of this letter without acknowledging the omission. The omission is indicated in brackets.

page 61:

> "Why worry so much about the future of a doomed world?"

We are unable to confirm Oppenheimer's original quotation. The quotation here is translated from Houellebecq's French citation.

page 65:

> Describing his first impressions of New York to his aunt, he claims he almost fainted with "aesthetic exaltation."

In the French edition, Houellebecq quotes at length from a first-person account by Lovecraft of his delight on seeing the New York skyline for the first time. However, neither Joshi nor I were able to find any evidence of this quotation in Lovecraft's writings. As a result, I have decided not to translate the passage, but have instead shortened it, reproducing the sentiment in the short sentence ("aesthetic exaltation") above. The French passage follows:

> *"J'ai failli m'évanouir d'exaltation esthéthique en admirant ce point de vue—ce décor vespéral avec les innombrables lumières des gratte-ciel; les reflets miroitants et les feux des bateaux bondissant sur l'eau, à l'extrémité gauche l'étincellante statue de la Liberté, et à droite l'arche scintillante du pont de Brooklyn: C'était quelque chose de plus puissant que les rêves de la légende de l'Ancien monde—une constellation d'une majesté infernale—un poème dans le feu de Babylone!*
>
> *"Tout cela s'ajoutant aux lumières etranges, aux bruits étranges du port, où le traffic du monde entier atteint son apogée. Trompes de brume, cloches de vaisseaux, au loin le grincement des treuils... visions des ravages lointains de l'Inde, où des oiseaux au plumage étincelant sont incités à chanter par l'encens d'étranges pagodes entourées de jardins, où des chameliers aux robes criardes pratiquent le troc devant des tavernes*

en bois de santal avec des matelots à la voix grave dont les yeux reflètent tout le mystère de la mer. Soieries et épices, ornaments curieusement ciselés en or du Bengale, dieux et elephants étrangement taillés dans le jade et la cornaline. Ah, mon Dieu! Qu'il fasse que je puisse exprimer la magie de la scène."

page 71:

> *"and all to the abhorrent discords of those mocking instruments. And then…"*

In French, Houellebecq includes here the phrase *"c'est alors que je me suis mis à trembler,"* which doesn't appear in any known English-language version of the story.

page 75:

> consonants that brought to mind certain proto-Akkadian dialects." Archeology and folklore play an equal part in the project from its inception. "We must review all our knowledge, Wilmarth!"

Niether S. T. Joshi, David Schultz, nor I are able to identify the exact text in these two paragraphs. The text in quotation marks is a translation of Houellebecq's French citation. Joshi writes: "We cannot locate any of these passages in Lovecraft's fiction. HPL never mentions 'proto-Akkadian' or 'North Carolina' in any of his fiction. The quotation about Wilmarth must come from 'The Whisperer in Darkness,' but that story makes no mention of Sumerian—nor does any other story." I have left these words, then, in quotations, indicating that they represent a quotation from a story:

> It is not just the clinical vocabulary of animal physiology and the more mysterious lexicon of paleontology (Archaean strata that have survived since middle Comanchian times…) that Lovecraft annexed to his universe. He was quick to understand the appeal of linguistic terminology: **"The individual, dark-skinned with somewhat reptilian features expressed himself with hooting emissions and rapid succession of consonants that brought to mind certain proto-Akkadian dialects."**
> Archeology and folklore play an equal part in the project from its inception. **"We must review all our knowledge, Wilmarth! These frescoes are seven thousand years older than the most ancient Sumerian necropolis!"** And HPL, ever impressive, slips in an allusion to **"certain ritual and particularly repugnant customs of the indigenous inhabitants of North Carolina."** But what's more astonishing is that he doesn't limit himself to the human sciences: He tackles the "hard" sciences as well; the most theoretical, those that are, *a priori,* the furthest from a literary universe.

page 77:

> a mythology that "would mean something to those intelligent beings that consist only of nebulous spiraling gases."

We are unable to find the original phrase by Lovecraft to correspond to Houellebecq's French: *"aurait encore un sens pour les intelligences composées de gaz des nébuleuses spirales."*

page 106:

> individuals of their background must not stand out by their speech or by any inconsiderate actions.

We are unable to find the original phrase by Lovecraft to correspond to Houellebecq's French: *"il n'appartient pas aux individus de notre classe de se singulariser par des paroles ou des actes inconsidérés."*

page 108:

> Where once he'd seen him as an elemental force called to regenerate European culture, he came to see him as "a clown," and then, to concede that although his objectives were fundamentally sane, the absurd extremism of his then-current policy risked leading to disastrous results that directly contradicted his original principles.

We are unable to find the original text by Lovecraft corresponding to Houellebecq's French: *"force élémentaire appelée à régénérer la culture européenne... honnête clown... bien que ses objectifs soient fondamentalement sains, l'extrémisme absurde de sa politique actuelle risque de conduire à des résultats désastreux, et en contradiction avec les principes de départ."*

page 109:

> great blond beasts of prey

We are unable to find the original phrase in the correspondence between Lovecraft and Long to correspond to Houellebecq's French: *"les grands bêtes blonds de proies."*

page 109:

> among the basest of species

We are unable to find the original phrase by Lovecraft to correspond to Houellebecq's French: *"de la plus basse espèce."*

page 115:

> What we detest is simply *change* itself

We are unable to find the original phrase by Lovecraft to correspond to Houellebecq's French: *"Ce que nous détestons, c'est simplement le changement en tant que tel."*

page 117:

hadn't fared too badly

We are unable to find the original phrase by Lovecraft to correspond to Houellebecq's French: *"pas trop mal tiré."*

TRANSLATOR'S BIBLIOGRAPHY

Arkham Collector No. 8, "Lovecraft on Love" (Winter 1971).

de Camp, L. Sprague, *H.P. Lovecraft, A Biography* (Doubleday, 1975).

Lovecraft, H.P., *The Call of Cthulhu and Other Weird Stories* (Penguin, 1999).

Lovecraft, H.P., *Lord of a Visible World, an Autobiography in Letters* (Ohio University Press, 2000).

Lovecraft, H.P., *The Thing on the Doorstep and Other Weird Stories* (Penguin, 2001).

H.P. Lovecraft, *Selected Letters 1911–1924* (Arkham House, 1965).

H.P. Lovecraft, *Selected Letters, Vol. 2, 1925–1929* (Arkham House, 1968).

H.P. Lovecraft, *Selected Letters, Vol. 3, 1929–1931* (Arkham House, 1971).

Matheson, Richard, *The Incredible Shrinking Man* (Tom Doherty Associates, 1994).

http://www.dagonbytes.com/thelibrary/lovecraft/theshadowoutoftime.htm

ACKNOWLEDGMENTS

It is thanks to Tom Luddy that I came to translate this book, and that it came to be published by Believer Books. In October 2003, Tom wrote an email to the editors of the *Believer* suggesting they acquire the rights and publish the first English-language edition. He had been turned on to it by the film director Barbet Schroeder, who had given it to him in Paris, telling him that it was the most brilliant of Michel Houellebecq's books. At the end of his email, Tom wrote, "Stephen King should do the introduction." Unbelievably, it has all come to pass!

In working on this translation, I was fortunate to be able to consult the erudite S. T. Joshi, the foremost H. P. Lovecraft scholar, who was generous with his time as he helped me uncover some of the more obscure references in Houellebecq's text. I am grateful to him.　　　　　*—Dorna Khazeni*

MICHEL HOUELLEBECQ was born on February 26, 1958, on the French island of Réunion. In 1985, he met Michel Bulteau, the editor of the *Nouvelle Revue de Paris,* who suggested that he write a book for the "*Infrequentables*" series, which had been launched at the publishing house Le Rocher. This led to the French publication, in 1991, of this volume, *H. P. Lovecraft, Contre le monde, contre la vie.* That same year saw the publication of *Rester vivant, méthode* (*To Stay Alive: A Method*), by Différence. In 1992, his first collection of poems, *La Poursuite du bonheur* (*The Pursuit of Happiness*) appeared. Maurice Nadeau published *Extension du domaine de la lutte* (*Whatever*), Houellebecq's first novel in 1994.

Houellebecq went on to contribute to many literary reviews in France. Since 1996, his work has been published by Flammarion, where Raphael Sorin is his editor.

In 1998, a collection of chronicles and critical texts called *Interventions,* along with *Les Particules élémentaires* (*Atomised*), his second novel, were published simultaneously. The latter has since been translated into more than twenty-five languages. In 1999, he collaborated on the screen adaptation of *Extension du domaine de la lutte* with Philippe Harel, who directed the film. That year he also published a new collection of poems, *Renaissance.* A book of photographs and text about Lanzarote, one of the Canary Islands, was published in 2000. *Plateforme* (*Platform*), was published in 2001.

Currently he lives in Ireland, near Cork. His latest novel, *La Tentation d'une île (The Possibility of an Island),* was published in France and the UK by Fayard and by Weidenfeld & Nicolson in August 2005.